A LAW UNTO MYSELF

By the same author:
No Mitigating Circumstances

A LAW UNTO MYSELF

Sir Neville Faulks

Formerly One of Her Majesty's Judges

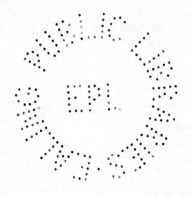

WILLIAM KIMBER · LONDON

First published in 1978 by
WILLIAM KIMBER & CO. LIMITED
Godolphin House, 22a Queen Anne's Gate,
London, SW1H 9AE

© Sir Neville Faulks, 1978

ISBN 0 7183 0086 6

Typeset by Watford Typesetters
and printed and bound in Great Britain by
The Garden City Press Limited,
Letchworth, Hertfordshire, SG6 1JS

To Elizabeth with love

Contents

Chapter		Page
I	As I was saying	9
II	Jasper	17
III	Liberace	26
IV	Counsel for Counsel	32
V	Geoffrey Lawrence	38
VI	Tommy Steele and Bruce Forsyth	53
VII	A Polish Military Hero	58
VIII	The Sound of Music	68
IX	The Case of the Chief Constable	80
X	Mr Mann and Dr Barbara Moore	88
XI	A Blow for Freedom	94
XII	Copycat Damages	104
XIII	One of the Faceless Fifty-three	112
XIV	Local Boy Makes Good	124
XV	In the Midst of Life	134
XVI	Tail-End Charlie	137
XVII	Family Multiplication	142
XVIII	A Winner and a Loser	156
XIX	Winged Words	163
	Postscript	177
	Index	181

List of Illustrations

facing page

The author,
  (by courtesy and flattery of Walter Bird)   30

'Papa', aged 90,
  by Edmund Nelson   30

Elizabeth, 1956,
  by Edmund Fearnley-Whittingstall   31

Major Tristram Kirkwood RE,
  Elizabeth's first husband   62

Elizabeth's second husband
  by Edmund Fearnley-Whittingstall   62

Elizabeth and Number Three, May 27, 1967
  'Do you really love me?'   63

Procession at Lincoln, 1972
  'I'd give him life'   126

Elizabeth and Jenny, 1964   127

Andrew and Jenny, 1958   127

Wallis's Cottage   158

Geriatric Occupational Therapy, 1977   159

Over half the family
  Elizabeth's Sixtieth birthday   159

CHAPTER ONE

As I was saying

I wrote much of this and the previous volume, *No Mitigating Circumstances* in the summer of 1974. Naturally many details have had to be altered and many amendments made with the passage of time. I was feeling unwell which I ascribed to overwork on my Committee on Defamation which seemed to have the effect of bringing on nasty and embarrassing nose-bleeds. I now know that it was not cause and effect, as I still occasionally suffer from this tiresome malady in 1977, which causes my brethren much innocent enjoyment as they contemplate me at luncheon toying with a piece of salad with a fork, wearing a large block of ice strapped to the back of my neck the while. I had to spend the winter and spring of 1974 on a peregrination of the North of England; Liverpool, followed by Leeds, followed by Newcastle. When we were at Leeds, I was having treatment for my psoriasis by the Emeritus Professor of Dermatology in that University, and overnight the knuckles of both my hands went out of shape, and the forefinger of my right hand swelled alarmingly.

I thought that it was gout, but it wasn't; it was psoriatic arthritis. Whatever it was, it wasn't doing me any good, and I was terrified that I should be unable to write as a result of a further swelling of the forefinger. My professor gave me a certificate saying that I needed a couple of months' rest and recuperation in a warm atmosphere, but by the time that I had soldiered on to Easter and returned to London from Newcastle I no longer felt like journeying to the mysterious Greek island which my wife Elizabeth had in mind for me, and was told, moreover, that I should be foolish to station myself out of reach of a medical adviser.

Thanks, therefore, to the Lord Chancellor's understanding kindness, I found myself in England with four months' leave (for August and September where my Long Vacation anyhow) during which to get ready for the next year's work.

'But what on earth are you going to do with yourself?' I was asked.

I thought, and said, 'Well, I shall spend most of it in bed,' and like a mug, I added, 'I daresay I shall write my memoirs. It will be good therapy for my hand.'

This piece of pomposity was immediately pounced upon by Harry Leon, who was known to millions as Henry Cecil, author of *Brothers in Law*, who happened to be in the room at the time. 'Good. Mine are coming out in a month or two. I'll give you some help if you like.'

And an ill-thought-out remark suddenly became a matter of amour propre, and I felt that I really must have a go. I had no idea whether I could write, or whether I had any interesting material to communicate, although I did have the advantage over him of having had a few years of glamour as a silk, whereas he by reason of his first wife's impending death had stepped into a County Court Judgeship from the junior bar.

Of one thing I was sure and that was, that, if I was to get my story down on paper at all, it had to be done at once, firstly because I did not know for how long my forefinger would be serviceable, and secondly because at sixty-six my powers, in the nature of things, could not be what they might have been twenty years before, and it was advisable to get on before they failed me altogether.

I pottered along for a bit, infesting the houses of various children and occupying their spare room beds. I had got as far as winning my scholarship to Uppingham and had quite enjoyed it, rather as a method of passing the time than as a creative effort, when Elizabeth came into the bedroom and said, 'Parcel for you.' I opened it and it was Harry's autobiography. The letter enclosed was laconic:

My Dear Neville,
                    Here's mine; where's yours?

That put me on my mettle (he would never have allowed me to write that, for he had an almost obsessive hatred for clichés), and I began to work rather than to play.

Harry's book and the fact that I still didn't know what was to become of me (the leeches had been very depressing), had the most remarkable effect. It was Dr Johnson who said: 'Depend upon it, Sir, when a man knows he is to be hanged in a fortnight, it concentrates his mind wonderfully', and he had a point there.

The words came boiling out like a geyser for three months and my hand became more and more painful until at the end of September, up in Argyll, I had finished.

Naturally enough a busy man like Harry would not read a holograph document, and I had to pay to hire a typist, to hire an electric typewriter, to buy vast quantities of typing paper, much of which I shall never recover from my friend, the very understanding taxman, because I am the sort of lunatic who never keeps receipts. Finally all was done – it had been infuriatingly hard work, for my writing is not very legible, and there was much labour involved in detecting misunderstandings, misreadings and misspellings.

Harry read it all in a week, and there was a great deal of it. The verdict was favourable, but, as I had expected, there were far too many clichés, it was much too long, and I must remember that it was 'only a first draft'. But, it had made him laugh; which was something. 'Only a first draft' indeed, and I had thought that I had put my all into it. However, he was the professional, and I the poor little dilettante, and I did, in a very minor degree, as I was told. I cut out some of the clichés, removed a number of the more boring personal anecdotes, preserved in their entirety all the professional stories, and underwent the hideous expense of re-typing.

I found a distinguished literary agent, and I sent him the 476 pages of typescript. He came to see me. He beamed.

'I read every word of it,' he said.

'I said to myself, 'I should certainly hope so. It's your job, isn't it?'

I was wrong. It was apparently a compliment, although I did not so understand it. These characters assimilate through skipping and could not possibly get through the pabulum dumped on their desks if they read it all as if it were Jane Austen.

He said, 'I gather that you want me to offer it to Kimber, as you mention him as your publisher?'

'Of course. I think that he is a splendid man. If he doesn't want it, you must advise me again.'

We parted, after he too had pointed out that there really was rather a lot of it, and I began to think that I should have to cut a substantial part of the book after all. This annoyed me as I am not as industrious as I was when younger, and I had thought that, having rather enjoyed writing it all down, nothing remained but to see if anyone would read it. After all, if they didn't, it wouldn't matter greatly financially; it would only be a blow to my ego, as the whole exercise was one of extroversion, a concept which is vicious rather than virtuous.

Time passed. At last came a signal that the good 'Peter' Kimber not only would publish, he would be generous as to advances, and, what was more, he would publish the whole perishing thing in two volumes so that the old gentleman would not have to make any cuts after all. So far, so good. But how was this fascinating autobiography to be entitled?

For myself, I had no doubts. No one has ever been able to pronounce my name. Now we will show them. First volume : 'Young Folks'; second volume : 'Old Folks'. It's as simple as that.

No sooner had I said the word, than murmurs of dissent were heard (Belloc, one of my favourites); it was much too flippant; it simply wouldn't do. And, of course, I gave in. I remembered how I had acquired a reputation for flippancy (entirely unjustly, to my mind) because I had a sense of humour, when at the Bar, and how it had nearly stopped my elevation to the Bench. It is sad how so many people cannot tell the difference between a wit and a jester. Danny Brabin, the dearest of men, was a jester; Bazil Wingate-Saul, my best friend, was a wit. Both from the Northern Circuit, the one a High Court Judge, the other a Circuit Judge, and both alas! now dead.

I remembered, too, how Mr Justice Rigby Swift said to Serjeant Sullivan, QC, who came over to this country in 1919, having become a marked man in his native Ireland for his support of law and order – for all that he had in 1916 defended Sir Roger Casement, in a stuff gown (as a junior barrister), on a charge of High Treason, at the Law Courts in the Strand – bringing with him, at the age of fifty, a wife, twelve children and a hundred pounds to start on his new career : 'Remember, Serjeant, the Englishman likes his law dull.'

The Serjeant, coming from the land of saints and scholars, where a basin-full of perjury matters nothing but to lack a sense of humour is dreary beyond belief, found this surprising, and his spirits rose when Sir Douglas Hogg, Quintin Hailsham's father, then Attorney-General, said about the late Lord Darling that he had demonstrated that to be wise it was not absolutely necessary to be dull. But in his book, *The Last Serjeant* the old gentleman confessed that Rigby's remark was certainly true. And he went on to say : 'I have known two members of the Bar in England to reach not only the Bench but the House of Lords solely by reason of their abysmal dullness. The English people regard it as a manifestation of profound wisdom.'

I wish I knew who those two were. One day, perhaps, Ted Megarry, the Vice-Chancellor (the Senior Chancery Judge), who knows everything, may enlighten me.

The grand old Serjeant; no one who ever saw this frail but indomitable bearded figure in court will ever forget him. His gimmick, and by George! it was a difficult one to sustain, was to have a very large brief (instructions from his solicitor as to the facts of the case) on the table in front of him, and to conduct the case with references to the pages of the correspondence while the red tape around his brief remained ostentatiously undisturbed. There lay memory and showmanship combined, and little boys, unemployed, listening to it, were delighted to see that he knew his entire case by heart.

One of his best and most well-known sallies was not original and was adapted from a riposte of another countryman of his. But it will do. Lord Justice Scrutton, a great friend, frail and bearded also, was foolish enough to inquire:

'But, Serjeant, has your client never heard of the maxim *Volenti non fit injuria?*'

To which came pat the reply: 'Sure, me Lord, it is the sole topic of conversation at the top of the mountain where my client dwells.'

Repulsed from *Young Folks*, I thought for a long while and then came up with *Struggle for Silk*, a reference to the fact that the first volume finally dealt with my attempt to gain from the Lord Chancellor a silk gown, (or the right to wear one, for he did not pay for it), which was indeed a struggle which I did not win until I was considered to be over the hill at fifty-one. Did that win favour? 'Not at all,' as they say in Ireland. The first person to whom it was put, thought that it referred to silk worms, and the second to a jockey. An odd sort of selection for a Gallup poll, I thought, but I retired again, and the titles have my approval but are not of my own choosing. After all, the publisher is not in the profession usually for philanthropic purposes and he must know better than the novitiate author what is likely to please.

My first volume ended with my appointment as one of Her Majesty's Counsel and perhaps therefore I should say a short word about 'Silk' which is the Rubicon between these two volumes of mine. Many a man has burnt his boats and regretted it. I was one of those who were lucky. 'Silk' is defined in *Chambers Twentieth Century Dictionary* without which, in my opinion, no household can be considered civilised (I am not a Scotsman, and no one has paid me for saying that) as 'the silk gown, or the rank, of a King's or Queen's counsel.' That is not very revealing, accurate though it may be. The silk is counsel for the Monarch in the sense that he is always available to act for the Crown.

But the practical point of his distinction, in my day, although this may shortly be abolished, was that he could not appear before Her Majesty's Courts without the assistance of a junior counsel who would then be entitled to two-thirds of his fee. In short, he was expensive. And, unless he was not only good, but very good, he was likely to fail, and to end by seeking some comparatively humble salaried job, in order to 'get his bottom on the Consolidated Fund' with a pension at the end.

And so I was very nervous when I went down to the House of Lords in April 1959 to be sworn in as a Queen's Counsel together with a number of others. What made me feel somewhat ancient was that while we were waiting, who should turn up in a whacking great limousine (we had come by taxi), dressed in ermine and looking, quite rightly, as pleased as Punch, but my old friend Harry Phillimore, ready to be sworn in as a Judge of the High Court, and years, but years, younger than I was.

The point was rubbed in still further when we took the oath in order of seniority. First was Kenneth Roberts-Wray, whom I had known as a child. He never really practised at the Bar, but was a very important civil servant with a GCMG. He must now be seventy-eight.

Next came Professor Wade who was a fellow of St John's College, Cambridge (where my father was an undergraduate), when I was an undergraduate. He never practised and must now be eighty-two.

Then Toby Humphreys, our Buddhist ex-Judge, who had been the leader of the Old Bailey Bar since 1950. He must now be seventy-seven.

And then, gentle reader, your author, twiddling the pennies in his pocket as he wondered what was to befall him. Was it to be the geriatric ward, or was it, just possibly, to be success?

We all took a very long oath, and then the Lord Chancellor burst in upon us. He was not beautiful, short, with that large very Semitic face which sometimes graces or disfigures the Scots. A look of jaundice about him. I did not know him. I had been told that

> The nearest thing to death in life
> Is David Patrick Maxwell-Fyfe

and I now understood what was intended. He delivered himself of a homily. A long homily, to which I had greatly looked forward, for he was a man of high reputation, but one which left me trying to pay attention rather than listening, disappointed as when a much advertised Divine has failed to stir his audience. Father Corbishley S.J. was such an one, unfortunately. All I can remember of this homily is that he ignored all of us, the practising barristers, and singled out for personal approbation two Conservative MPs, Sir Knox Cunningham, who did not practise at all, and Peter Rawlinson who had become a Member of Parliament at the age of thirty-six, and who, at thirty-nine, was the baby of the Party. He was right, of course, to make suitable remarks about Peter, who was, in fact, at the beginning of a most distinguished career – although how Lord Kilmuir knew that, I wonder – but the whole address revealed that this was a politician, who was wholly out of touch with what went on in his profession in London to which, as a Northern Circuiteer, he was really a stranger. In Wales he was always known as 'Dai Bananas'. I don't know what it means, but I think that it was very appropriate.

Whereas the High Court is closed during the Long Vacation except for Vacation work (which nowadays can be quite substantial), the Central Criminal Court at the Old Bailey, which seems to get a few more days off at Whitsun than we do in the Strand, is open throughout September. This was a good thing for me, for I had a nice big prosecution to conduct for the Board of Trade, which was remunerative without being particularly difficult. It was the last time that I appeared at what had been my stamping ground for a dozen years, and, when I was asked to luncheon there recently, I didn't recognise the place.

When I started to practise there in the thirties the judicial team consisted of a High Court Judge, sent down from the Strand to try the murders, the Recorder, Sir Ernest Wild, who, when there was no crime to try, would sit in the Mayor's and City of London Court dealing with civil matters, the Common Serjeant, Sir Henry Dickens, son of Charles Dickens, who really ought to have been Recorder in the general opinion, and the Commissioner, Sir Holman Gregory, who eventually became Recorder for a short time in the teeth of opposition from Sir Henry Curtis-Bennett.

Those who have read Marjoribank's marvellous life of Marshall-Hall, an advocate who would have been hopelessly out of fashion today, will remember that he, like Curtis-Bennett, nourished a desire for the Recordership, but in vain. And I remember poor Derek, Curtis' son, telling me that he had not the least desire to be a High Court Judge, spending 'most of the year sleeping in somebody else's bed', but that the Recordership of London would be marvellous, endless City dinners and always at home. It didn't come off for him either. Tony Hawke, who died before he should have done, was often against me in my food cases after the war, was Senior Treasury Counsel (which meant that he prosecuted the murders), became Chairman of London Sessions, the job that old Curtis-Bennett had had to accept, and eventually came back to the Old Bailey as Common Serjeant, and subsequently Recorder. I was there when the Bar welcomed him back. He was nearly in tears, and it is astonishing how much nostalgia that forbidding old building can engender.

After the war Gerald Dodson, the Recorder, was fully employed and one or two extra judges were sometimes called upon to help out.

Now there are sixteen or so judges permanently employed there, and it is not a case of 'the Red Judge', for there may be three High Court Judges sitting down there at once. It is indeed an indictment on the behaviour of our times.

CHAPTER TWO

Jasper

I was in the middle of my Board of Trade case when the newspapers were full of the sensational departure for Israel of a solicitor called Grunwald, who was thought to have absconded with millions of pounds belonging to the State Building Society. He had in fact gone to Israel, but he hadn't taken any great sum with him. He and a man called Murray were a brilliant couple who were determined to become very rich indeed. Grunwald at the start was poor and Murray was rich, but mere riches were not enough for him. The more he had, the more he wanted. The basic theme was like that of the office boy who puts his hand in the till to get the money to play the horses, wins and puts it back, takes a lot more from his employers, loses the lot, and goes to gaol. The till was the money of the State Building Society of which Murray was the Managing Director and Secretary. He used to spot valuable property, buy it for himself with the assistance of Grunwald who looked after the legal niceties, and sell it on to the State Building Society, who had unwittingly provided the money for the original purchase, and pocket the substantial profit. Of course if Murray had been an indifferent valuer and had bought property other than at a bargain price, it would have come to light much sooner that he was speculating with the Building Society's money for his own benefit. But these two were astonishingly successful for a very long time, and they only came to a sticky end, like the late Clarence Hatry, by 'over-egging the pudding'. If Murray had only raided the till once more, they might well have got away with it.

Grunwald had been brought to this country shortly before the war in order to avoid Nazi persecution. His benefactor had been a Rabbi called Schonfeld to whom he turned again for help when he left the country on 13th September 1959. He sent the Rabbi to the South of France to Murray, crying for help. The furore was occasioned by the fact that it had been discovered that £3,255,000 of the money deposited by the public with the State Building Society had been paid to Grunwald on 29th July 1959. That was in relation to a scheme for the purchase by Murray and Grunwald of Dolphin Square, then the largest block of flats in Europe, on the Chelsea Embankment. The cry for help was occasioned by the fact that Grunwald had over-reached himself by arranging a scheme, almost at the same time, for purchasing the Ely Brewery Company Ltd where the ruling spirit was the flamboyant Mr Lazarus Nidditch, whom I had come across in other earlier litigation.

Unfortunately for him, in neither transaction did he succeed in raising quite enough money to pay off all the shareholders who had accepted the offer for their shares, and it was the incomprehensible failure of Mr Murray to provide a further £700,000 from the State Building Society towards the purchase of the Ely Brewery Company Ltd that caused the takeover to fail and precipitated Grunwald's flight. He, like Jabez Balfour a century before, appeared to be a very religious man, and spent a great deal of his gains helping Bulgarian Orthodox Jewish refugees. There had been a great many successful take-over bids before this, in which it had not been noticed by the public that what was happening was that the money to provide the purchase price of the particular quarry was coming out of the quarry's own assets. This was contrary to the provisions of Section 54 of the Companies Act 1948, which, however carried a maximum penalty of £100, so that anyone who wished to breach it could not care less. (I recommended that teeth be put into the section, but of course nothing was done, but when, eighteen years later, Mr Slater of Slater, Walker was prosecuted (and acquitted) under it, the newspapers expressed their surprise at the prescribed penalty.)

The other actor in the play was Mr Harry Oscar Jasper, born in Berlin on 19th December 1904, who had also left Germany, then with the surname of Jaspis, for this sceptred isle which sometimes overdoes its charity.

He was induced by the other two to lend his name to all the take-over bids, and, in the result, the public knew nothing of Grunwald and Murray, the men who mattered, but read about Jasper, the financier. Indeed, Mr Macmillan, at that time Prime Minister, made an urbane reference in the House of Commons to the Revelation of St John the Divine, chapter twenty-one, verse nineteen which, as every schoolboy knows, reads:

The first foundation was jasper; the second, sapphire; the third, a chalcedony; the fourth, an emerald; the fifth, sardonyx; the sixth, sardius; the seventh, chrysolite; the eighth, beryl; the ninth, topaz; the tenth, a chrysoprasus; the eleventh, a jacinth; the twelfth, an amethyst.

The spotlight was accordingly upon Mr Jasper and, while I was at the Old Bailey, Bobbie (now Sir Robert) Speed, then Solicitor to the Board of Trade, came down with several acolytes and told me that 'by order of the Board of Trade dated 25th September 1959 made in pursuance of their powers under section 165 (b) of the Companies Act 1948, Mr Neville Faulks QC was appointed to be an Inspector to investigate the affairs of H. Jasper and Co. Ltd.' I was very grateful to him. I then for the first and only time in my life underwent the full press treatment. For a very short period I became a public figure.

'Politicians all over the country joined in what had now become a dramatic election issue,' said the now defunct *Sunday Dispatch*. Why it should have been such an issue I did not understand, not being a politician like Mr Macmillan and Mr Gaitskell. Some of the publicity was distasteful and some was amusing. Undoubtedly, it was good for trade.

The Press were polite and considerate and I suppose they published what they thought the public wanted. There was a photograph of the Chief Superintendent of the Fraud Squad going into my back door by mistake (or perhaps to avoid the press), and another of me in my back garden taken presumably from a helicopter. The public were told that my dog was called Paulo and that my daughter was told to stop playing chopsticks on the piano in order that I could concentrate. The offender was in fact my sister Lorna and the animal was called Paul, but no matter.

It was even worthy of report that I caught the 9.06 from Earlswood to Victoria every morning, and crowds were alleged to have been waiting to see me walk in the procession from Westminster Abbey to the House of Lords on the occasion of the opening of the Michaelmas Law Sittings. This seemed to me to be rather over-egging the pudding, as the photograph in the newspaper showed me invisible beneath a full-bottomed wig, and a very small crowd indeed.

Then there was tremendous excitement about Mr Grunwald's movements. At one moment he was going to come back from Israel, and the next moment he wasn't. So I thought that, as at any rate at one press conference he had been reported as saying that he would talk to me in Israel, I should go out to Haifa and do so. We had no satisfactory mutual extradition treaty with Israel at that time. I went to Petty France to deal wih passport technicalities and was dogged by a reporter and it was all in the press.

This produced a sweet letter from an anonymous lady :

To Mr Neville Faulks, Queen's Council (sic)
Sir,
   Just an ordinary woman following up your case and worried concerning your visit to Jerusalem. I implore you, sir, to take a detective or two and several gentlemen also with you, knowing as I do that that that city has for some years been turned into the old-time city of refuge. My reason for this warning is nervous that you, if alone, will not come out alive and there is a lot of trickery still in them and keep you own group and self together all the time. I have been thinking that they want to buy firearms to fight against Egypt. Sir, lawyer that you are, you will never argue them in their own country. Quentin Reynolds, Victor Gollancz, 'Let my people go', but if you have not seen the painting of them under Pharoah at the Guildhall before today sir, do so, sir.

Respectfully yours,
A Woman.

I will only quote one other, anonymous again, and written in capitals.

TO MR. NEVILLE FAULKES (sic) Q.C.
ASK MR GRUNWALD ABOUT THE DIAMOND JEWELLRY (sic) AND FUR COATS HE BOUGHT HIS WIFE, WEEKS BEFORE HE WENT TO ISRAEL.

I never had the opportunity to ask him about these irrelevant matters in Israel, for he suddenly announced to the press of the world that he was coming back to England to submit himself for cross-examination. This seemed almost too good to be true for I had no desire to leave my home and family for an indefinite period, but it was so. He came home after I had seen Mr Maxwell Joseph, who was concerned with Dolphin Square but whose behaviour in the matter had been quite beyond reproach. He received a lot of publicity which I greatly regretted, and which must have been unwelcome. I hope that he will forgive me for mentioning his name.

Mr Grunwald came to see me as soon as he landed, and was incredibly co-operative. I took his passport away and put it in my drawer and began to cross-examine. It was unnecessary. My first remark was, 'Now would you like to tell me all about it?' And he did, for days and days. When I wanted documentary corroboration of anything, the file was always forthcoming, and when I caught him out in a forgery he admitted it and wept, whereas he could have blustered and baffled me, for I am no handwriting expert.

On 10th October 1959 the newspapers had two front page items: (1) 'Conservatives have majority of 100' and 'Rush to buy shares' and (2) 'Grunwald charged with $3\frac{1}{2}$ million fraud'. I was working separately from the police and I was not pleased when I read this latter item. He had been arrested as he left my chambers. I had known nothing about it, and felt that the very special relationship of the confessional which existed between us must have been jeopardised. But not a bit of it. They gave him bail and he returned to tell me more of this very complicated system of buying companies and paying them the purchase price out of their own assets. When I mentioned his weeping, that was not meant to be offensive: he was emotional as were all the Orthodox witnesses, and tears were by no means unusual. After all, I myself cannot hear 'Land of Hope and Glory' without recourse to tears.

I conducted the enquiry by having one witness at a time with a solicitor to hold his hand, if he wanted one, and a shorthand writer to take down what transpired. The shorthand writer, whose name I forget and should not have forgotten, was a marvel. The transcripts were ready in no time and gave me the ammunition I needed. For after a few days I became convinced that in Grunwald we had that unusual figure, 'the sinner that repenteth' and I was prepared to believe all that he said and use his evidence to cross-examine others.

I concluded that Murray had no intention of telling the truth, but Grunwald's evidence was corroborated in part by that of his partner, a Jewish solicitor whom I did not consider to be involved in the fraud. By the time that I had been going for a month the whole floor of my room was littered with files of the various 'Jasper' companies and files of various earlier property dealings completed before the property in question was ever unloaded on any of the puppet companies.

Murray was such a fantastically brilliant appraiser of the value of real property that he could have made his million quite respectably from the legal point of view without getting into trouble. But he was greedy. One of the bits in my report originally read, 'Murray was elderly, unscrupulous and rich; Grunwald was young, unscrupulous and poor. They were made for each other.' I was pleased with this, and so was David Hirst, (now QC) whose help was invaluable, but it somehow got bowdlerised and paragraph 27 of the Report lost its punch.

I enjoyed all this very much, and by dint of keeping long hours – I was in chambers until nearly midnight one night and had to catch the milk train to Reigate, a daunting experience which I took care not to undergo again – I got on very quickly with the report. Mr Jasper and his partner obligingly contradicted themselves on a vital matter, and I had to spend very little time with them. Perhaps I was getting a bit too big for my boots, for I told David that I would write the report and set out the facts, and he could write an addendum dealing with the various civil and criminal liabilities of the dramatis personae. Quite apart from the fun for him, I thought that he, having been last at school, would be more likely to get it right.

And the poor boy flogged away and in the end produced a document very nearly as long as, and much more erudite than, my report. I dictated my part into a Grundig, and had to be careful of my words as, although I knew how to stop it, I was not very mechanically minded, and could never remember to press the right button to obliterate anything of which I disapproved.

I was appointed on 25th September 1959, and, exhausted, I sent the final typed report to the Board of Trade on 1st December 1959. A substantial document, David and I thought, and we waited for popular acclaim, the bottom having dropped out of our market once the election was over.

But that was not to be. Bobbie Speed came and told us that all David's handiwork would have to be ditched. It wasn't our job to recommend prosecution, but merely to report. The Director of Public Prosecutions (who subsequently made a real dog's breakfast of the case) should do that. 'Very good, sir,' I said, and took out half the report.

(In the long run all that unpaid work didn't do David, who was devilling for me, just as I did for Gerald (see *No Mitigating Circumstances*) any harm. He now has the most colossal practice as a QC, and is a Fellow of his old school, Eton College.)

Then it was decided that as Grunwald, and by this time Murray and Jasper, had been arrested the matter was sub judice and my report should not be published at all, lest the jurors be prejudiced when they came to try the case. It was delightful to think that the hypothetical juror would read the report of an inspector appointed by the Board of

Trade in accordance with the provisions of Section 165 (b) of the Companies Act 1948, and distinctly flattering – but not very convincing.

Then the trial came on and Murray and Grunwald went to prison for five years. They had been charged with the fraudulent application of cheques, in one case amounting to £150,000, and in another to £3,255,000, belonging to the State Building Society, for purposes other than the purposes of the State Building Society – and in other counts for, having received the cheques, fraudulently converting the proceeds to their own use and benefit. Jasper was acquitted. He was in my view a fortunate man. We had recommended that he be charged with obtaining money by false pretences, a charge to which I thought there to be no defence. The late Morris (Mr Justice) Finer, who defended him, told me that he would have advised him to plead 'guilty' to such a charge. But the DPP (not Sir Norman Skelhorn but his predecessor) decided not to prefer the charge!! He had his company's and his personal licence to deal in securities revoked, however; he told the press that he had been adjudged bankrupt, and perhaps that was enough. He was very small fry, and also engaging company in cross-examination, even when putting both feet in it.

This method of arriving at the truth is the nearest thing to the Inquisition that prevails under our law. By seeing all the witnesses separately, and in one case unexpectedly, I was able to elicit the truth without any chance of the witnesses trimming their evidence to accord with what others had said, which would surely have occurred had the proceedings been held in public. Sir David Napley has written to *The Times* to disparage this procedure, however, and he is an exceedingly experienced criminal solicitor.

The one unexpected case was that of Mr Cow, the Chairman of the State Building Society, in his late seventies, once a collaborator of Murray in the purchase of properties, but now a puppet.

The Press gave much publicity to the fact that he was returning with his wife to this country on the *Queen Mary* from a holiday in America, and, subsequently, to the fact that on arrival at Southampton, he had declined to speak to the Press, as of course he was entitled to do.

One Saturday morning, after a thoroughly exhausting week, I was thumbing through the local telephone directory for some unremembered purpose, when by chance Mr Noel B. Cow stared out at me from the pages with an address nearby in a flat at Lord Rank's old home. It was tempting to play *An Inspector Calls*, but he was an old man and I rang up, ascertained that he was also the right man, and made an appointment to see him the next day. He was very scared, very charming, very co-operative, and I hope that I managed to reassure him. He had told a number of lies to shareholders, but I was quite satisfied that he was wholly under the thumb of Murray, who had probably drafted his speeches. When accordingly I came to see Murray for the second time, I had some more material to put to him.

Although it is very dramatic to call on your neighbours in this way, I don't recommend it, for you have no shorthand writer; you can't spoil the cross-examination by saying, 'wait until I write that down', and you have to go home and write it all down while it is fresh in your memory. The decent thing to do is to get it typed and send it off for signature, with the danger of having a lot crossed out. Whether I did that or not, I forget.

After I had finished the Jasper enquiry, I was appointed Inspector of one of the companies in the Jasper 'empire', the Pilot Insurance Company. Happily, I had an expert actuary, Mr R. K. Lockhead, to inspect with me. He did most of the work, and I remember very little about it, for by this time, unexpectedly, I was getting really busy.

Gilbert Paull of the Tracy case (see my first volume) had become a High Court Judge and presided over my first case in silk. This was sent to me by Mr Herbert Baron who has recently written to *The Times* to say that if Lord Hailsham can bring in a bill to ensure that a Roman Catholic can be Lord Chancellor surely he can add a little clause saying that the same applies to a Jew. I have sympathy with that. It is a difficult problem that has been with us ever since Lord Haldane, as a junior, was asked to advise whether constitutionally the first Lord Russell of Killowen, then Lord Chief Justice, could become Lord Chancellor, and I imagine that the present unopposed bill is meant to accommodate Sir Peter Rawlinson. But it would seem silly if the first Marquess of Reading could be Attorney-General, Viceroy of India, and Foreign Secretary, but was constitutionally debarred from the post of Lord High Chancellor. I haven't looked up the law and it may be that Mr Baron was making a bad point. No one has bothered to answer him, probably because the Act of Settlement was only directed against Roman Catholics.

Gilbert Paull also tried Murray and the others and told me afterwards, with some smugness, that of course he hadn't read my report.

I wondered why on earth I had been asked to undertake this very onerous and not very well paid chore. Eventually the Report was published, as a very damp squib indeed, on 19th June 1961, more than eighteen months after I had submitted it.

But I make no complaint, for the advertising value of the publicity brought in a lot of work and enabled solicitors to consider me as more than a mere defamation specialist, while a number of newspapers described me as an experienced commercial lawyer, which was flattering but untrue. If they had said that I was experienced in commercial crime they would have been right, but I did not take *Scrutton on Charter-Parties* to bed with me, and my knowledge of the Hague Rules was minimal.

CHAPTER THREE

Liberace

The only case which was heard in the summer of 1959, before I began the Report, which was well advertised was that of Liberace where I was led by Gerald Gardiner as, although I was now QC, I had started the case as a junior.

Inevitably, Gilbert Beyfus, who was coming to the end of his Indian summer, was for Liberace, leading Buster Milmo who was still a junior.

The article of which complaint was made had been written by Bill Connor who, under the pseudonym of 'Cassandra', had written the leaders in the *Daily Mirror* for many years. This was a Labour newspaper and Cassandra's outspokenness during the war years had not been palatable to Churchill. Nevertheless, he was a figure nationally known, to whose views much attention was paid, and his distinction had been officially recognised when he died as Sir William Connor. He produced the following vitriolic attack upon the plaintiff.

I have to report that Mr Liberace, like *Wunderstarke Funf*, is about the most that man can take. But he is not a drink. He is yearning-wind strength five. He is the summit of sex – the pinnacle of Masculine, Feminine and Neuter. Everything that He, She or It can ever want. I spoke to sad but kindly men on this newspaper who have met every celebrity arriving from the United States for the past 30 years. They all say that this deadly, winking, sniggering, snuggling, chromium-plated, scent-impregnated, luminous, quivering, giggling, fruit-flavoured, mincing, ice-covered heap of mother love has had the biggest reception and impact since Charlie Chaplin arrived at the same station, Waterloo, on September 12, 1921.

This appalling man – and I use the word appalling in no other than its true sense of 'terrifying' – has hit this country in a way that is as violent as Churchill receiving the cheers on V.E. day. He reeks with emetic language that can only make grown men long for a quiet corner, an aspidistra, a handkerchief and the old heave-ho. Without doubt he is the biggest sentimental vomit of all time. Slobbering over his mother, winking at his brother, counting the cash at every second, this superb piece of calculating candy-floss has an answer for every situation. . . .

Nobody since Aimée Semple MacPherson has purveyed a bigger, richer and more varied slag heap of lilac-covered hokum. Nobody anywhere ever made so much money out of high-speed piano playing with the ghost of Chopin gibbering at every note. There must be something wrong with us that our teenagers longing for sex, and our middle-aged matrons fed up with sex, alike should fall for such a sugary mountain of jingling claptraps wrapped up in such a preposterous clown.

The questions were whether what Connor had written was fair comment, and further whether the words in their natural and ordinary meaning meant that Mr Liberace was homosexual.

As to the latter point, I must have been one of those exceptionally innocent or unworldly persons to whom the Judge referred in his summing up, for it had never occurred to me that Connor meant that. However, the jury did think so, and, as we didn't appeal, I must accept that they were right and I was wrong. The Judge, who is a man of the world, eventually stated that on the question of law, he had come to the conclusion that the words were just capable of the meaning which the jury had found, although he was by no means certain that he would have come to the same conclusion of fact.

When the jury came back, a middle-aged female juror, of the age group to which the plaintiff was said to be most attractive, gave him a wink before the foreman announced the result. I said to Gilbert, 'Did you see that?' The old boy grinned. Not very satisfactory though.

We had a forceful opening from Gilbert which took us to lunchtime. He told the jury movingly how his client had been born in 1919 in Milwaulkee, Wisconsin, and was the son of an Italian immigrant, (a French-horn player named Salvatore Liberace), and of a lady born in the United States of Polish parentage, who was a concert pianist before she married. From his very birth, he declared, Mr Liberace had music in his blood.

(In fact he was and no doubt is a very talented entertainer. I should not have known this if I had not been instructed by the *Mirror* to sit through a vast number of recordings of his television performances. He was not for me, and I am quite sure that old Beyfus would not have been entertained, but everyone is entitled to his own taste, and I am sure that he has given very many middle-aged women much innocent pleasure.)

Bridget was in court to see the fun, and at the luncheon break, Hugh (now Lord) Cudlipp asked us to eat with his party. I don't like having luncheon with the client, although it is sometimes unavoidable, but when Bridget said, 'Do let's', I expressed my gratitude and agreed. Hugh seemed to have taken over most of the Devereux public house and some minion of his must have been very busy organising matters, for we were fed with the most splendid collation, to which I did justice, assuring myself that I should not have to open my mouth that day.

Most of Fleet Street seemed to be there, and Bridget enquired whether that wasn't Malcolm Muggeridge. She was told that it was, and was asked if she would like to be introduced. She would, and she was. I was in an anti-Muggeridge mood at the time, as he had made some remarks about the Royal Family which had annoyed me more than somewhat (although in no way approaching the Willie Hamilton of the present day) and I remained seated. She returned, thrilled, and I was pleased with that.

Gardiner was not there. He very sensibly was polishing up his cross-examination as it was possible that he might have to start that afternoon for there was not very much for Liberace to say in examination in chief. However, Gilbert drew it out, and Liberace did not finish until the next day. Then ensued the most brilliant cross-examination, all straight out of the head, without a note, and at the most tremendous rate which must have left the jury stunned. And not a smile! Bang! bang! bang! like a machine gun. But Liberace had a bullet proof garment on, and I felt that it was all to no avail.

'What about Semprini?' cried Gerald (who had a great admiration for that artist of whom I also knew, as he lived at Reigate).

'Who?'

'Semprini.'

'Never heard of him.'

It didn't work. There was a short re-examination, and another witness was called, Liberace's manager, full of tedious financial details. He finished, and Gerald leaned over to me, 'You take him,' he said dejectedly, 'you've got a lighter touch than I have.'

I was prepared to accept that, but it was short notice, and how to be light about transatlantic expenses I did not know. So I got up and said as blandly as I could, 'My learned leader thinks that we should have a change of bowling to see if we cannot get a quick wicket before the close of play.'

That went rather well, and the witness, who of course was baffled and hadn't understood what on earth I was talking about, was tolerably co-operative and I played out.time without mishap.

Next day I was told to exhibit my well known light touch by taking on Miss (now Dame) Cicely Courtneidge and Mr Bob Monkhouse. I managed to get the latter to give the jury an example of his impression of Mr Liberace, after some stern words from the Judge, but although it lightened the atmosphere (always keep it light with the jury if you think you may be going down, for the damages will be much less) I scored nothing at all. Nothing either with the Dame, who told me, when she came to luncheon with Jack Hulbert at the Nottingham Lodgings in November 1973, that she had been very nervous, and didn't really know Liberace at all well. Unhappily, she didn't appear nervous, and I assumed that she did know him well, and I missed my opportunities.

When our side gave evidence, poor Bill Connor was a surprisingly inept witness. Just as the editor of *The Sunday Times* had been foolishly suspicious of me in Miss Tracy's case, so here he fenced with Gilbert quite unnecessarily, not giving straight answers and failing to do himself justice. Sensible of this, Cudlipp then proclaimed that he wished to testify. We had no proof from him, but his evidence in chief didn't really matter. If the old master couldn't resist the challenge to cross-examine him, he hoped somehow to improve the position. Gerald, without batting an eyelid, duly took him through a quarter-of-an-hour of near irrelevancies, and tendered him for cross-examination.

Gilbert, who had no need to cross-examine at all, took the bait, and a very entertaining hour or so ensued. It was mainly to do with the general attitude of the *Daily Mirror* and a particular cartoon in its sister newspaper the *Sunday Pictorial*. Hugh Cudlipp gave as good as he got, and found the centre of the stage to his liking. Gilbert also obviously enjoyed himself, and, so I would think, did the jury. I certainly did. But, when it was all ended, the euphoria dispersed as we came to the speeches. The Judge would be bound to say that most of this was irrelevant, and indeed he did.

The only thing that I can remember about the final speeches was that Gilbert, in the old tradition, told the jury how extremely ably Gerald had conducted the case for the newspaper and for Mr Connor. Gerald who had spoken first did not have the opportunity of saying *tu quoque*. And the Judge took it up.

(It was Mr Justice Salmon, who had been made a judge on 2nd May 1957 and was already very much in the public eye for his severe, and rightly severe, sentencing of the Notting Hill mob who had started a race riot. I was in court, waiting for a notorious Stock Exchange fraud trial at the Old Bailey to begin, when he pronounced the sentences. I have never taken life too seriously, but I was very impressed on that occasion.)

The Judge told the jury in the Liberace summing up : 'I would like to say that you and I have been privileged to hear an outstandingly forceful and brilliant example of advocacy from Mr Beyfus, who is a master of the art, one of the outstanding advocates of these times. His performance was characterised by his usual extreme fairness.' That must have pleased my old friend.

There were two libels alleged. The jury found for the newspaper on one, but against us on the other awarding £8,000 of which £2,000 was said to be attributable to the allegation of homosexuality.

There was nothing at all in the summing up of which complaint could be possibly made. Indeed, it leaned towards us rather than to the plaintiff, but with that woman on the jury and the general prejudice against newspapers it is not surprising that we lost. When I wrote an opinion to the effect that we had four good points for the Court of Appeal, the *Mirror* would have none of it. They didn't say why, but I am not wholly unsophisticated.

The trial must have sent up the sale of the paper. All those photographs of the gorgeous plaintiff and all the blow by blow reporting of the various cross-examinations ! But the deliberations of the Court of Appeal on intricate matters of defamation law would be of no interest to devotees of Miss Marjorie Proops.

The Cudlipp hospitality has not been abated by our failure in this case. Very often since then Hugh and members of his hierarchy have nobly held a 'Liberace Dinner' at Kettner's at which Cyril and Jeannie Salmon, Elizabeth and I, and once, when Lord Chancellor, Gerald Gardiner have attended. Bill Connor, alas, only came to one.

I heard no more of Liberace for many years after the case was over and was amused to read a snippet in *The Times* in 1974 :

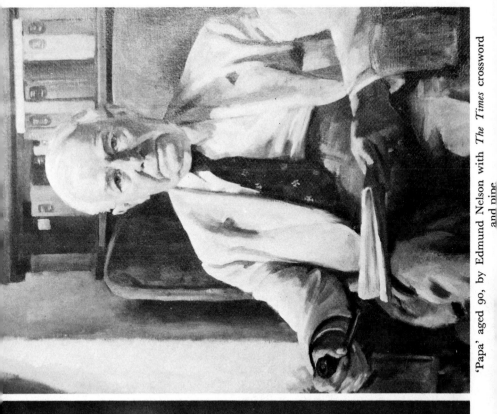

'Papa' aged 90, by Edmund Nelson with *The Times* crossword and pipe

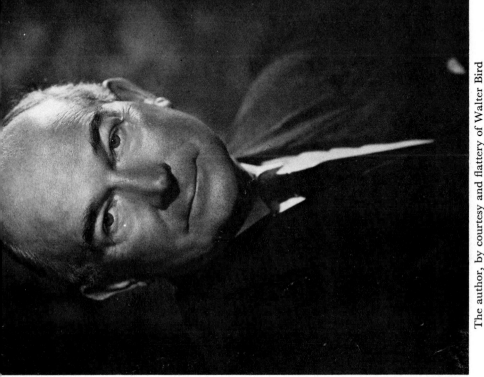

The author, by courtesy and flattery of Walter Bird

Elizabeth, 1956, by Edmund Fearnley-Whittingstall

Los Angeles. 15th January

Liberace, the pianist, who is 54, is being sued for 1,500,000 dollars (about £700,000) by a former chorus-girl, who claims she was defamed by his published account of their romance.

Miss Joanne Rio Barr, aged 38, claimed that the book implied she was Mr Liberace's girl friend, had been unchaste, and had used their relationship for her own pecuniary gain.

Will it be the 'biter bit'? I hasten to add that I know nothing about the merits of the case, if any.

CHAPTER FOUR

Counsel for Counsel

After I had finished my report on the Jasper Group of Companies it was only three weeks before Christmas, and only seven before I should be fifty-two years of age. If nothing else had turned up by that time I should have begun to worry. But my good fairy, in the figure of Gerald Gardiner, had been at work. He had, as the then 'top boy', been retained in some libel actions in relation to the Gordon Hotels. They owned the Mayfair Hotel, The Metropole Hotels at Monte Carlo, Brighton and Folkestone, and held a long lease of the Grosvenor Hotel at Victoria Station. It then transpired that one of the libel actions was being brought by a Queen's Counsel, who was complaining of a couple of letters sent to the Secretary of the General Council of the Bar, alleging professional misconduct against him.

Gerald Gardiner was the Chairman of the General Council of the Bar, and felt that he could not be involved in the case. The solicitor for the various plaintiffs looked round in despair. Possibly because I had some time before appeared at the Old Bailey, led by Mr (later Sir) Milner Holland QC, on behalf of Mr Leonard Percival Jackson, the managing director and general Pooh-Bah of the concern, who had got into trouble for making a false statement to the shareholders of Gordon Hotels Limited, I was given the brief. I did know of Miss Zena Daniels, who had led the faction which opposed Mr Jackson, but not a great deal more. I certainly knew nothing of the intensely complicated matters which were to engage my attention by day, while attempting to finish Jasper by night.

My client in the first of these actions, which was tried by my original benefactor, Gerald Slade, and a jury, was Roger Keyes. I found that Milmo was to be my junior. He didn't seem to mind, but it was somewhat embarrassing, as he had been busy at the libel bar before my time. I remember Fred Lawton in similar circumstances more or less apologising for having been briefed by the Board of Trade to lead me at the

Old Bailey. There was no need to apologise. Mr Justice Barry, a dear and sympathetic judge, who was not a first class lawyer, any more than I am, had acceded to Frank Soskice's (now Lord Stow Hill) arguments, and misdirected a jury on the question as to whether the prosecution had to establish a criminal intent for there to be a conviction under a regulation concerning hire purchase. There had been an acquittal as a result. The prosecution can't appeal from an acquittal, and the only thing we could do was to prosecute somebody else under the regulation, when the same point would arise and we might have a strong judge who would refuse to follow Mr Justice Barry. We had such a case already committed for the next session at the Old Bailey, with the inevitable Gerald Gardiner for the defendants. I hadn't taken silk and Fred just had. It would be a good start for him, and, after all, there was absolutely nothing he didn't know about crime, and we had much respect for each other. We found Mr Justice, now Lord, Diplock waiting for us at the Old Bailey and, as he was and is a first class lawyer, there was a conviction, which was upheld by a very strong Court of Criminal Appeal.

Fred still leads me, for he is now in the Court of Appeal, where he has recently got into trouble with *The Times* newspaper for saying in a judgment that a certain section was pregnant with pitfalls. I imagine that the trouble was that he didn't tell us whether the pitfalls were destined to be twins or triplets. But whereas *The Times* may be sound on its mixed metaphors I nearly wrote some years ago to point out that the front page headline, 'Dubcek to meet with Brezhnev' was not English but American. Colin Duncan told me I would be a pompous ass if I did, and I didn't. We all make mistakes.

When poor Bridget died suddenly in May 1963 of virus pneumonia, after we had been married for twenty-three years, dear Fred did something which I shall always remember. On the Sunday between the death and the funeral, he asked my father, my daughter and myself over to luncheon at Purley because he suspected, correctly, that we should have no Sunday joint, as there would be no one to cook it.

That gesture as well as the innumerable kind letters I received did a lot to help in a difficult time. Roger Keyes, whose case I am about to describe, came to the funeral.

He is the second Baron Keyes of Zeebrugge and Dover. His father is part of history, and his elder brother won the Victoria Cross and was killed in the last war. He had served in the Royal Navy from which he retired, going into the City, and becoming Chairman of Mappin and

Webb, the jewellers, and of Dannimac, manufacturers of raincoats. He lived at the material date at Benenden Place, in the village my connection with which was to lead to my second very happy marriage in 1967.

That material date was 22nd December 1957. He was just about to leave the house, for the purpose of ringing the bells for Matins at the village church, when he received a momentous telephone call. It was from a gentleman who had introduced himself earlier in that month as the solicitor to the 'shareholders committee' of Gordon Hotels Ltd. of which the secretary was Miss Zena Daniels, who had received some publicity as a racehorse owner. This man had said that the committee was anxious to be free of Mr Jackson, and also of a pair of American brothers. He added that Mr Ashe Lincoln QC, whom Roger had met once, had agreed to be vice-chairman, and that that gentleman had suggested that Lord Keyes should be chairman.

This was flattering, and he accepted, on terms that he should have his complete independence guaranteed in writing, and further that he should not sit on a board with Mr Jackson. It then transpired that the American contingent had called a meeting for 30th December, and he agreed to be elected a director on 23rd December, Mr Jackson to be removed on the 30th.

The momentous telephone call was to the effect that on the previous night the 'shareholders committee' had come to an agreement with Mr Jackson, and Lord Keyes was required to visit the Daniels' establishment in Highgate forthwith in order to discuss the matter.

Arrived there, he found that on 30th December the shareholders' committee would not help the Americans to get rid of Mr Jackson, who would be persuaded to retire peacefully at an early date, as the committee 'had him over a barrel'.

(Mr Justice Cassels told the jury in the third action that he had tried to imagine what this must be like, and he supposed that it must be very uncomfortable.)

Roger Keyes met Mr Nutt, the chairman of the shareholders' committee, who eventually became the first defendant in the first action, and agreed to allow his name to go forward for election if guaranteed (1) that Miss Daniels would retire after three months and (2) that Mr Jackson would retire at an early date and (3) that his independence on the board would be assured. Freed of these two conflicting factions, and the Americans not having got on to the board, he thought that he and Mr Lincoln could save the company. These two accordingly were elected directors on 23rd December, the Monday, and the five other directors included Miss Daniels and Mr Jackson.

On 30th December he was elected chairman and Mr Lincoln vice-chairman, and learned for the first time that Mr Jackson had a controller's agreement which was said by the solicitor to be unbreakable. High words were used and Mr Daniels, the father of Zena to whom he used to refer as 'my little sputnik', and who was not a director, said of the so-called independent chairman, 'If that bloody lord doesn't do as I tell him, I'll kick him out and become chairman myself.'

Things went from bad to worse, and eventually a circular, signed by Mr Nutt and printed and published by Finchfort Publishers Ltd of Eastcheap, was sent to the shareholders dated 2nd April 1958 making violent accusations against the chairman and vice-chairman. There is no point in repeating the libel. Miss Daniels was the sole director of Finchfort Publishers Ltd. at the date of the circular, but said she had nothing to do with it, although she thought that a draft from which the circular was made was in the possession of somebody on her side. I had opened the case to the jury that, although the hand was the hand of Nutt, the voice was the voice of Zena, so that that answer did not satisfy me. The Judge joined in by pointing out that she was the only person who could have forbidden her company to print the libel.

She became excited and shouted, 'Can I say who wrote the circular?'

I answered, 'Say anything you like.'

She pointed dramatically across the Court: 'Counsel wrote this circular . . .' (and she named him).

It was her junior counsel – her leading counsel, a charming man who is now a circuit judge, having left the case during the cross-examination of the plaintiff. This was very theatrical, and counsel did not deny it, saying that he had drafted the circular on oral instructions and 'several documents had been before him'. He did not, from counsels' seats, tell us who gave the oral instructions, or what the documents were and I could not cross-examine him. I will not mention his name: he has now left the Bar.

There was too much ill feeling in the case for it to be enjoyable. We sat every evening until 6 p.m. in the hope of finishing in time for Gerald to go to Leeds Assizes. It must have taken a terrible toll of him as he commuted to and from Beckenham daily, and was so meticulous that he would never dream of going into court without having carefully read and re-read his voluminous notes of the previous day's proceedings.

Even so the case lasted twenty-three days, and the plaintiff was in the witness box for forty hours.

Roger was the most terrible taskmaster. He would ring me up in bed at Reigate Heath in the morning with some new points which he had just remembered as ammunition for the cross-examination of the next enemy witness, meet me at the barrier at Victoria Station, take me to his bedroom in the Grosvenor Hotel, and then drive me to the Law Courts, holding forth all the while non-stop, and I couldn't say 'Leave it to me', for it was all good stuff, and the complexities of the matter were such that it would not have been possible for any solicitor to put all these minutiae in the brief.

Eventually the jury found the libel to be untrue and that both Nutt and Finchfort Publishers Ltd were malicious. Mr Nutt was ordered to pay £35,000 and Finchfort £35,000 jointly with Nutt plus another £5,000 for publication of the libel to *The Financial Times*. Lord Keyes remained chairman of Gordon Hotels Ltd. It was a resounding victory but I doubt if the plaintiff ever recovered anything like that sum. Finchfort were impecunious and the twenty-three days' costs on top of £35,000 damages must have been too much for Mr Nutt unless he was very well to do indeed, or unless the 'shareholders' committee' helped him out.

The only time that the Judge smiled during this painful case was when I had to rise to my feet to say that in the previous week I had said to the jury that Miss Daniels was as full of malice as a Stilton cheese was full of maggots. This piece of hyperbole had brought down upon me the wrath of the the Stilton Cheese Manufacturers Association, to whom I offered an unreserved apology for any imputation against the quality of their product, which I was sure was uniformly maggot-less.

That wasn't enough for the unsmiling cheesemakers, for the next day, apart from the report in *The Times* which, in those days, never missed anything even mildly entertaining, another national newspaper carried the following letter :

Sir,

I was most surprised to read in your issue of November 26th a statement by Mr Faulks in the Lord Keyes libel case, as follows :

'You know that Zena Daniels was as full of malice against Lord Keyes as the best Stilton is full of maggots ?'

This statement was reported without comment ! I am sure that you, sir, know, and I would have thought learned counsel would have known, that the best Stilton is neither full of, nor does it contain, any maggots. It would not be a best Stilton with a single maggot in it.

Yours faithfully,

Secretary,

Stilton Cheesemakers Association, Melton Mowbray, Leics.

Since then I always lie down in the car when we go through Melton Mowbray, Leics!

No young, or at any rate, very junior silk complains if he has a lot of work, but by the time I had laboured for many days in May 1960 in another case in which Lord Keyes sued Mr Daniels, who appeared in person to defend himself, I felt that I had had enough of the Gordon Hotels. The jury in that case awarded £6,500 damages. Then I spent from 14th June to 24th June 1960 haranguing a jury on behalf of Mr Ashe Lincoln QC in another action against Mr Daniels, who this time appeared by counsel. The jury awarded Mr Lincoln £7,500 damages.

Then both Nutt and Finchfort appealed against Lord Keyes. It took a very long time and they lost. Then Daniels appealed against Lincoln on the ground that his libel was absolutely privileged (as indeed it would have been if it had been a statement in Parliament). That went on for about a fortnight and the Court of Appeal upheld Mr Justice Salmon and Daniels lost.

That, mercifully, was the end. They did not try to go to the House of Lords.

CHAPTER FIVE

Geoffrey Lawrence

Geoffrey Lawrence died young after being a High Court Judge only for a year or two. He was much loved. When I came back from the war he was the leading junior on the South Eastern Circuit. He lived in Sussex and his brother was the Under-Sheriff at Lewes. He branched into Parliamentary, town planning, and rating work to great financial advantage, for it is generally better to appear for a body of persons than for an individual, however well-to-do. But this type of work gains little publicity, and Geoffrey's name did not become a household word until his successful defence of Dr Bodkin Adams on a charge of murder.

He was faced by the Attorney-General, leading the present Mr Justice Melford Stevenson, and he took the incredibly daring decision not to call the doctor as a witness. Mr Justice Devlin's summing up on this point is well known ('you prove it I don't have to explain'), and the defence triumphed. I was involved in one or two defamation matters after this, with the doctor as plaintiff, and my impression is that they were reasonably compromised without the doctor being too greedy.

Once, of course, he had got into the public eye in this manner, Geoffrey became number two at the *cause célèbre* bar to Gardiner, followed the latter as Chairman of the Bar Council, a task he discharged with brilliance, making, they tell me, a much better speech than President Eisenhower, when the legal profession went to America in 1960 as guests of the American Bar Association, and generally widened the scope of his work. He had always had a substantial divorce practice of the better class sort but, as only the judgment may be reported in such matters, the general public did not know how good as well as courteous a cross-examiner he was, more in the school of Birkett than of Hastings.

It was in a matrimonial case that I first crossed swords with him. This was alarming, for although I had done a number of routine un-defended divorces as a junior, I had never done a defended nullity case in my life. And I was a rather simple creature to whom the whole subject was rather unpleasant. When I was at school I thought that the verb *amo* meant 'I adore', as in those deathless lyrics for an American chorus at some revue at the Ambassadors in the forties:

> Amo, amas, I love my Latin class,
> Amo, amas, amamus; Teacher's the cat's pyjamas.

It wasn't until I was about sixteen that I came across the 'Pervigilium Veneris', as I think it was called, the song before the Saturnalia, and realised that that basic word also meant 'I make love'.

> *Cras amet qui numquam amavit,*
> *Quiqui amavit, cras amet.**

And, being a smug little boy, I suppose, I didn't think much of that advice.

It is strange to think that this case, where, as the innocent, I took on the practised hand, was one of the very few which I can remember where, in winning, I believe that I was party to a miscarriage of justice.

Defenders of criminals must have that experience often, but, then, I was never regularly a defender of criminals, and an unmerited acquittal is merely one in the eye for the establishment. To feel that you have been party to depriving someone of what in your heart you consider to have been their legal rights is not a pleasant sensation, and I worried a lot about it, especially when the wife did not appeal. But it had a happy ending.

Geoffrey, whose junior is now a judge, appeared for a young and beautiful wife whose husband was represented by me, and by a junior who is now dead. The husband was a rich man who could afford to live in style without doing anything very much to justify his existence. He was a lot older than the wife whom he had met on the hunting field when she was a 'land girl'. Her background was respectable but impecunious, and she was overcome when he took her to Glyndebourne and showered her with presents. She agreed to marry.

Not long after the wedding, the parties became unhappy and eventually she put in a petition alleging cruelty and saying that the husband could not consummate the marriage. Her case of cruelty was substantial, if it were true, but of course in these cases, unless there are black eyes

* *Cras* means 'tomorrow' as in procrastination).

and that sort of thing, it is generally word against word, as an intelligent villain will only be cruel to his wife in private.

Her case of nullity, however, was to be dealt with, in part at any rate, by the report of a Medical Inspector approved by the court, whose duty it was to inspect and report to the court about both parties. It seemed that the learned and very experienced Judge had read the report, which the Inspector would be called upon to substantiate in evidence, and which strongly favoured the wife's case without actually expressing a conclusive opinion. Accordingly he said, 'Mr Lawrence, I have only considered your case of cruelty on paper and I must say that I have seen stronger. On the other hand I have noticed what Doctor ——, who is so very well known and highly respected in this court, has to say. Do you really think you want to go on with the cruelty which will consume a great deal of time?' Geoffrey was reluctant, but considered discretion to be the better part of valour, and the case of cruelty was thrown out of the window, much to my gratification.

Then we were all asked to go and see the Judge, who perfectly properly asked me if I really wanted to continue to contest the issue of nullity, in view of what Doctor —— was apparently prepared to say. I said that indeed I did so wish as my client's case was that there had been intercourse not once but many times and not only during but before the marriage.

On that defiant pronouncement we returned to court and battle was joined. The Inspector was called first so that he could get away to his practice. He was so ancient that I wasn't surprised to have been told 'he is very well known in this court' etc. I didn't think him at all an impressive witness, but of course it was not what I thought but what the Judge thought that mattered.

Then the wife went into the witness box where she remained for a very long time. She stuck to her case that there had never been inter-course, (and I believed her), but conceded that there had been 'heavy petting' in the same bed before marriage which I fancied caused a slight elevation of the judicial eyebrows. She admitted that on one occasion she had lied to her husband when she was going out dancing with another man. This was of course perfectly understandable if the husband had been treating her with cruelty at the time. To summarise, as a result of a long and tiring cross-examination, she made a number of admissions, which could be damaging, or which could express her absolute candour, according to the approach of the Judge.

I felt that I had had a hard if not wholly unsuccessful struggle when the court rose. Then Geoffrey came across to me and said that the wife had just told her solicitor that on one solitary occasion she had had sexual relations with another man after the ceremony of marriage. She had not thought it important to mention it, but Geoffrey – and he was an honourable man of course – thought it his duty to tell me. The matter would have been relevant had the cruelty charge been persisted in, for then it would have been postulated that there had been a valid marriage, and there would have been a matrimonial offence on her part, which the Judge in his discretion would have overlooked, if he felt that there had been cruelty and that the solitary peccadillo was excusable. But if the wife was right and the marriage was no marriage because it had never been consummated, then the one act was not adulterous and was irrelevant. Except, that is, as to the husband's contention that there had been frequent intercourse.

A further inspection might help to support or to qualify the evidence already given by the Medical Inspector. I suggested this and Geoffrey could not but agree as, fortunately for me, he had asked the Judge not to sit on the following day for his convenience, as he had to do a rating case in the Court of Appeal, and I had readily agreed. So this poor wretched girl had to be inspected again. I am not going into anatomical details as she will recognise the case (and I hope no one else will).

The question then was whom we were to choose to set up against the Medical Inspector, if his conclusions should chance to differ from those expressed by this ancient and trusted dignitary. I remembered that the late and great Dr Aleck Bourne lived not far from me in the country, and I besought Messrs Gordon Dadds and Co., who were about the most efficient solicitors in the business, to get on to him. They did and he was prepared to give an opinion. He was a very distinguished gynaecologist who had years previously leapt into brief celebrity in the 'Horse with the Green Tail' case. In that matter a child of fourteen had been beckoned into the quarters of some of our brutal and licentious soldiery, so that she might see their horse with the green tail. She did not see the horse but became pregnant instead. Abortion was a crime and Bourne was a man of compassion. He knew what he was doing, and was satisfied that what he was doing was right. He removed the unwanted foetus and was tried at the Old Bailey. He encountered that greatly underrated judge, the late Mr Justice Macnaughten (affectionately known as 'Muggins'), and was acquitted.

If he came before my Judge and gave the evidence I wanted, I felt that his national renown, even though he had now retired, might be too much for his very well known and highly respected senior. And thus it came about. My client blustered away in the box; I didn't believe him although I had no grounds for so feeling, and Geoffrey did not score. Then Dr Bourne told us that what he had found accorded entirely with both what the wife said and with what the husband said. He added that he wasn't present at the earlier inspection, but with great deference to the Medical Inspector it seemed probable that he would not have arrived at the conclusion that she was *virgo intacta* at the time. Geoffrey told me afterwards that once Bourne had said this, he knew that he was finished. And so it proved.

If he hadn't wanted to do that case in the Court of Appeal, and if I had not been instructed by very efficient solicitors, and if Dr Bourne had not had time on his hands, having retired, and many other ifs, that case might have gone the other way and I think that it would have been the right way; for I just believed her and I didn't believe him.

The unlucky girl went off and got a job looking after the horses, oddly enough, of an old friend of mine. The husband continued his bachelor life.

Years later, I met my friend and enquired after the girl, for I had her on my conscience.

'Oh, I thought I'd told you. It's all rather splendid. He's dead, and he forgot to alter his will, so she's got the lot.'

'God works in a mysterious way his wonders to perform.' That's what the Vicar was supposed to have said that we would sing in the event of a Liberal party majority, but this anecdote gives it point.

Some months after I wrote this last passage I was in the provinces exercising my Family Jurisdiction. One day I disposed of a suit which had been compromised. It took very little time, and the principal thing that I noticed was that the female petitioner (Mrs Z) was very well-dressed. Three days later I met my old friend whose horses the unsuccessful petitioner in the nullity case had looked after. I asked him about her. 'Oh! you gave her a divorce last week. Mrs Z, you know.' I am ashamed to say that I did not recognise her. And to add to the coincidences, when my friend said that, the poor girl's original junior counsel was sitting in the next room.

Geoffrey's emergence to the centre of the stage caused us to be against each other in a defamation matter which went to the House of Lords. He didn't know much about the technicalities of defamation, but he could pick anything up, and he had a very clever junior, who will be a judge one of these days. [October 1977 : he has just become Mr Justice Hodgson.]

The case concerned a distinguished public figure, who has since been knighted, about whom my newspaper, this time the *Daily Mail*, had said something defamatory based on some observations made by a Member of Parliament in the proceedings of a Select Committee or something of that kind. There was no doubt that the plaintiff was jealous of his very high reputation and was very upset at what had been said about him. Indeed he wept in the witness box while I was cross-examining him, which was very embarrassing for everybody. There were a number of defences, which I had drafted when I was a junior, one of which was that we said that the words were not defamatory, but if they were we were very sorry. When we got to the Court of Appeal I couldn't be there to take the reserved judgment, but David Hirst told me that the Senior Lord Justice had made a good pun by referring to this plea as a piece of *faux bonhomie*. I congratulated the learned Lord Justice by letter, only to receive an apology saying that he never intended to refer to me at all. Better had I not written.

My newspaper had paid money into court on my advice. They weren't very keen on that usually, but on this occasion I managed to persuade them that the whole case was a question of 'how much?' and that a payment in was useless unless it was realistic. I said that I knew from experience that you wanted to pay a little over the obvious figure as a judge and even a jury might think it good to beat a hypothetical payment in. And they paid £2,100 into court.

We had Mr Justice Pearson, now retired as a Lord of Appeal in Ordinary as Lord Pearson. He listened with great patience and almost in silence and eventually delivered a long and most impressive judgment.

Before the case opened I was told by my clerk that Geoffrey wanted to see me. He was my senior in silk and it was for me to go to him. He suggested that I paid £7,500 and indemnity costs. I told him that, whereas in those days the *Express* might pay rather than have bad publicity, my newspaper would usually fight, so that blackmailing writs would be discouraged. (There was of course no question here of a blackmailing writ or we should not have paid a lot of money into court.)

At the end of the day the Judge found that one article was not defamatory, but that in the other the plaintiff had been seriously defamed. He found that there had been a very ample clearance sixteen days later and that the newspaper had not been malicious. He awarded £1,100 damages. We had beaten that by £1,000 and the plaintiff got £1,100 with costs up to the date of payment in, and we got the costs thereafter. If that had been the end of the matter, the plaintiff would have been well out of pocket. The case had come on the week after the first Keyes case and I was exhausted, and disappointed to hear that the plaintiff was to appeal.

The whole point about a payment into court, I should perhaps explain, is that it is a bet. 'I bet you don't get more than that,' and the Judge has no idea what is in court.

You may imagine the indignation of the newspaper when it appeared that the transcript furnished for the Court of Appeal contained all the argument about costs which followed the award of damages and revealed to all and sundry the exact amount that we had paid in. It was of course wholly illogical that the Judge at first instance should award his damages in the dark, but that in the re-hearing in the Court of Appeal a different principle should prevail, and the three wise men should know exactly what was in court. And when within five minutes of the opening of the appeal Lord Justice Sellers said that with a man in such an important position the damages seemed far too small, poor Dennis Walsh, my solicitor, became more or less apoplectic. When he could speak, he said, 'We've had it' and we had. The presiding Judge said that he concurred with the assessment of damages of his two brethren at £4,000 although his own unaided assessment would have been somewhat higher.

We went to the Lords and lost again. It was little consolation that the damages did not amount to the £7,500 Geoffrey had asked for, because it would have been cheaper in the long run to have settled on his terms.

When it was all over I wrote to the then Master of the Rolls, Lord Evershed, pointing out the anomaly of having a secret payment in the court below, and having an open payment in the Court of Appeal where the matter is theoretically a re-hearing with three judges instead of one. I received a courteous but useless answer. He had consulted his colleagues and they were of the opinion that knowledge of the amount paid in in no way inhibited their ability to do justice.

Of course it didn't, but I had to explain that to the newspaper and it wasn't easy. One would have thought that it was obvious that, as Lord Hewart said, justice must not only be done but be seen to be done.

I am a bit of a terrier in some ways and I took it up again after I had become a judge with our new Master of the Rolls, Lord Denning. He wrote to say that he entirely agreed with me but that he was not sure of the views of his fellow members of the Court of Appeal. Nothing happened for some years. Then at last he made a pronouncement which has stopped the practice of shorthand writers revealing the amount of the payment in; and I am satisfied.

The last matter where Geoffrey's path and mine crossed, rather indefinably, as silks (for he led me several times as a junior), relates to the rather strange practice of the giving and receiving of retainers. Retainers are of different kinds, a retainer for an individual case, a retainer for a particular type of case, or a general retainer. My experience has been that they don't do counsel any good, but can be very valuable to the client. The practice arises from the fact that etiquette says that we are all on the taxi rank and must accept the first passenger whether or not he is wearing a collar and tie. If a potential plaintiff wishes to instruct Mr Y, the well known defamation practitioner, to act for him in proceedings against the *Daily Chronicle*, however, it is quite proper for Mr Y's clerk to say that he is very sorry but he cannot accept the instructions, as Mr Y has a retainer from the newspaper.

'Retainer' means that for a sum of £2.10 for a junior or £5.25 for a silk (the figures may have been altered since my day) the client undertakes to employ the counsel either always in a special type of case, in a particular case, or generally as the case may be, at an appropriate fee, and counsel for his part undertakes not to appear against the client. If the client defaults and employs someone else, counsel is said to be entitled to demand a brief in the case none the less. Such demands were often made in the last century, but it is an embarrassing matter and I don't recall it ever happening in my time.

When I was given a retainer by a newspaper, which I would understand to relate to defamation matters only, it had a prestige value but no more. They would presumably have briefed me anyhow, while by paying a small sum all at once they secured that I would not appear against them. But it can be annoying and I will only give two examples.

I had not long been in silk when I received a general retainer from the late Mr Nubar Gulbenkian, millionaire and litigant. We took the five guineas with pleasure. The next thing we knew was when we read in *The Times* that Nubar was having a splendid action against the BBC and was employing Sir Lionel Heald QC as his leading counsel. An excellent choice, but a breach of contract. Lionel Hawkins my clerk, and I shrugged our shoulders and said nothing. But the fact is that if the BBC had asked him if I would lead for them, as they might have, he would have been bound to have said that he was very sorry but I had a general retainer for the plaintiff.

In the second case I was given a retainer by a firm, of whom I had never heard, to lead for the defence in a libel action to be contested between Mr Randolph Churchill and Mr Nabarro MP. The retainer was accepted as we thought it might be rather fun.

Randolph Churchill had been in a libel action before this when the *People* had called him a 'hack' or words to that effect which are obviously offensive but difficult to justify as they are so mercurial in meaning. The same trouble as that which we had encountered in Liberace. Churchill used to go to Colin Duncan in my chambers whom I had known since I was nineteen. Against the *People* Colin had been led by Bill Fearnley-Whittingstall who had started his final speech to the jury with the words, 'Yo! Ho! Ho! and a bottle of rum' which, no doubt for excellent reasons, found favour with them, and a substantial sum of damages was awarded.

But now Bill was dead. And the plaintiff went to Gerald Gardiner. Mr Churchill was a man of determined character and no doubt he had decided for himself, and rightly so, that Gardiner was the man for him. But if he or his solicitors had asked Colin or our clerk if they had any idea whom they would like to lead, they could not have mentioned my name as I had a retainer for the other side.

Time passed and the case appeared in the Warned list for the next set of jury trials. No brief. Finally my clerk rang up only to be told that Mr Nabarro had also retained Mr Geoffrey Lawrence QC, that he had gone down to the House of Commons and asked his cronies which counsel he should have, and they had told him to have Geoffrey. My clerk spluttered a bit, but the character at the other end of the telephone apparently honestly had thought that you could immunize all the leaders of the Bar at £5.25 a time, and then take your pick. So we shrugged our shoulders once more and did nothing about it. It didn't matter financially, as I dare say I had some dreary case in the Restrictive Practices Court that I could fall back upon, but it was annoying. I was looking forward to the cross-examination, because, whereas I have forgotten what Mr Nabarro had called Mr Churchill, I knew, and I am very sure that Geoffrey didn't, that I had collected a lot of money for a distinguished journalist whom Randolph Churchill himself had been misguided enough to call a 'hack', and who didn't mind having a little extra money to spare Churchill having to make a public apology. That cross-examination was not to be. But perhaps it was as well; for *The Observer* said, 'Geoffrey Lawrence who had the dreadful job of facing up to cross-examination by Randolph the other day. . . .' (6.11.60)

The other big case that was going on at that time was also one in which enquiries were said to have been made for my services, but I had no retainer. My clerk rang me up at home and said, 'Rubinstein Nash have been on to me about a consultation. Something about *Lady Chatterley's Lover*. I told them you were off to America and they could have a consultation when you were back.'

I cursed under my breath. But it was no good being cross. When I came back, Gerald Gardiner had got the brief, and he was again the right man. I would not have had my heart in it, and to parade a lot of our intelligentsia to say that this well known novel was 'in the finest Puritan stream of English prose' would not have appealed to me.

*

As we had had a disastrous caravan holiday in 1959, when it transpired in 1960 that we were invited to the United States, with lots of lovely hospitality, we accepted with alacrity. We knew that we would have to go as poor relations, because, when the Americans come here, they can put it all down against tax and have a long weekend in Paris into the bargain, while for our part the Revenue makes no concessions. However, we had had an unexpectedly profitable year and the Bar Council had arranged a cheap Atlantic flight, as well as hospitality for us in Washington, Richmond (Virginia), Atlanta and Chicago. Those were the places that we put our names down for, and as neither Bridget or I had ever been to America before, we were excited at the prospect. We gave the Bar Council all the information that they wanted and looked forward to the trip enormously. We were only sad that, when last the American Bar Association had come to England, our offer of hospitality at June Farm had been rejected as being too far from the metropolis.

The Bar Council's plan was to match up the hosts and guests according to their age and seniority in the profession. And when we were told that our host in Washington was Mr Joseph P. Finkelbaum (that was not his name – but not far off), we pictured a genial middle-aged musicologist.

We started from Heathrow in a rather suspect looking DC10 (or it may have been a DC7) which immediately made Bridget have kittens as to whether we should reach Montreal. It was Montreal to which we were going, for although the American Bar Association welcomed us and the President himself was to show us hospitality, bureaucratic America was being horrid and refused to allow us to land in New York. Heaven knows why! But the route was to New York via Montreal. That was apparently all right.

We arrived at Shannon safely, if in discomfort. Bridget kept saying that there was something wrong and I unkindly said that we had lost one of the engines, but would make the Atlantic on the other. No sooner had we left Shannon than my idiotic remark proved true; there was an irregular sound as we proceeded, and then we turned back for Shannon with Bridget holding my hand very tightly. It appeared that a meal was available in the airport restaurant but also that it would almost certainly be oversubscribed. I don't like pushing, and would almost certainly have given up the struggle, but Bill Mars-Jones, now Mr Justice Mars-Jones, pushed us forward and with characteristic flamboyance informed the first waiter that he saw that I was the Lord Chief Justice of England, and that my party must have precedence. There was nothing that I could do about it, and we received VIP treatment.

We were also initiated by Professor Hanbury into the mysteries of Gaelic coffee, which Bridget seemed to find very acceptable. This was as well for it enabled her to sleep through most of the endless journey ahead, and although we did not know it, alcohol was not to pass our lips again for a very long time. My chief recollection of our noisy and overcrowded journey is that there was only one lavatory and there seemed to be endless queues of distinguished lawyers and their wives waiting throughout the night to make use of its facilities.

Eventually we landed at Montreal where the temperature was over 100 degrees, and we were left to languish for more than an hour. How we envied Sheila Mars-Jones who, being allergic to flying, was crossing the Atlantic in the *Queen Mary*. At last our captain was heard to shout that his party would frazzle unless something was done, and a de-hydrated, prematurely aged body of persons climbed down to the burning tarmac. The reception arrangements were fairly primitive, although Bridget managed to get a glass of water. I had no such chance as we were immediately called for our flight to New York. Arrived there, of course it was the wrong airport from which to leave for Washington. We were all bundled into overcrowded omnibuses. Poor Lady Russell who was holding on to a stanchion was shouted at, 'No standees' and she sat down hurriedly. Such violence to the English language upset me considerably, so that I may not have been in such a low physical state as I seem to recollect.

Spirits began to rise as at last we approached Washington just over a day late and there were a number of people awaiting our arrival. Couple after couple left the aeroplane to be greeted by their hosts until there were only the two of us and poor Mr Boulton, now Sir William Boulton, the greatly overworked officer of the Bar Council, who was in charge of our travel arrangements. He had business to attend to and soon we were alone, tired and depressed, but with no idea what we were in for.

After what seemed a long time Mr Joseph P. Finkelbaum appeared, aged about twenty-two, with forty-eight hours' growth of beard on his face. He complained about the number of our suitcases. I understood why, when we staggered outside to be confronted by the only, and very old, Ford Anglia which I saw in the United States.

He was kind enough to enquire if we had had a meal. We had not, and he took us to what in England would be called a 'teashop' nearby, where children were buying sticky cakes. We both wanted to wash and descended a number of stairs into a subterranean chamber, where the arrangements left much to be desired. Emerging, we each had a bun and a beverage which looked not unlike tea but I think that he said that it was made out of the bark of a tree. It was not appetising but I was so thirsty and hot – I have since learned that Washington is said to be at its worst in early September – that I had two glasses.

Mr Finkelbaum then told us how sorry he was to have been so late, and explained that he was in great trouble. He and his wife had parted but she remained in the apartment and we couldn't go there. However a friend and client had offered to help out by providing us with accommodation. We said how kind it was of his friend, and we re-entered the Anglia. I sat in the back with the bags, in some discomfort, and Bridget, who was looking very tired, sat in the front. I did my best to keep the conversation going with inane remarks about Kennedy and Nixon, as it was election year. He drove on and on.

'Is that the Gettysburg Memorial?'

'Yes: you don't know how difficult it is for a Jew to get any work from the insurance companies here.'

'Oh dear! is that so?'

'It is', and off he went into a long diatribe. Poor boy, he felt that the world in general, as well as his wife in particular, was against him.

We drove on and on and soon were out of Washington.

'And what does your kind friend do?'

'He sells newspapers.'

'Oh yes! Where?'

'From his shop. Sometimes on the corner.'

'Oh!' and I added, 'Oh! yes, of course' to sound more democratic.

On and on we went, Bridget taking no part in the conversation.

We stopped somewhere in Maryland in a street lined with bungalows up from the sidewalk. We stumbled up with suitcases, and opened the front door to see Dad and Mom and four children watching television. They were kind and hospitable, and offered to show us our room off the living room. It had two bunks in it, one above the other, which two of the children had kindly vacated for us for the night.

I shut the door, leaving Finkelbaum to talk to his client. Bridget said, 'America!' and started to sob. I tried to quieten her and persuaded her to have a shower (there was no bath). Then she said in a tone of despair, 'That's not my suitcase', and it wasn't. It belonged to Professor Hamson of Cambridge University, the very distinguished jurist, who had presumably taken hers by mistake.

Finkelbaum, poor boy, was kindness itself. He would go back all the way into Washington and effect the exchange if it was the last thing that he did. And he was as good as his word. By the time he returned, Bridget was asleep in her bunk half dressed, and I had discovered that, entirely owing to my own stupidity, I was unable to shave as I had failed to obtain the appropriate adaptor for my electric razor. I was grateful to him for collecting the case and even more so when he said that he would bring me his spare electric razor in the morning, which I could mail to his office before I left Canada on my way home. I asked him what we should do in the morning. He said, 'Well you can't expect these good people to give you breakfast when they've done so much,' and arranged to fetch us early.

I took a note of our address (which I have now forgotten) in case I could find some alternative accommodation, and he drove us right into the centre of Washington, not far from the hotel where the activities of the British group were to be co-ordinated. We had breakfast at what in England would be called a 'Good Pull-up for Carmen' by which I mean that the surroundings were scruffy but the food was quite all right. Then we parted, and Bridget and I walked to the hotel ready to 'tell all.'

No one was in the least interested. The hard-worked Bar Council officer had to listen, and, when I had finished, he said that he thought that there were two beds left in a dormitory at Georgetown University, but he couldn't really recommend them. Everyone else was happily making arrangements about their next point of call *after* Washington as the majority of them had been there for two days already, having shunned our confounded Dakota.

I said to Bridget that, rather than be entirely in the hands of this nice boy, whose parents we might just conceivably have been, for she was thirty-nine and I was fifty-two, I would try the Imperial Tobacco Company for help. I knew that they had offices on the other side of the river.

Then someone tapped me on the back and said, 'Oh! Mr Faulks, I admire you so much.'

I didn't know who he was, but I said, 'Good, I'm flattered; but do you think you can find my wife and myself somewhere to stay in Washington? We've been let down.'

To my surprise he replied, 'Oh you poor people! I think I may be able to do something. I act for Gulf Oil.'

My benefactor, whom I have not seen from that day to this, was Mr Laszlo Gombos, a partner in Theodore Goddard and Co, over in Washington to lecture on the Common Market, or the Treaty of Rome as it was then called. His 'admiration' was apparently caused by his having wandered into court to listen, when I appeared for Lady Winchester against Mrs Fleming on the instructions of his firm (see *No Mitigating Circumstances*).

We arranged to meet later in the morning. It must have been still quite early because, when I rang up the Imperial Tobacco Company, I was frustrated to find that they were not in Washington DC but in Virginia where the time was one hour later, and they weren't yet open. Eventually both Imperial and Gulf came up with an apartment with room service, kitchen, deep freeze, and I know not what else, at the Roosevelt Hotel, and we were saved.

The next event was another rescue operation, that of our baggage. I left Bridget in the Bar Hotel with a kind and understanding female member of the English Bar to hold her hand, and sallied forth, feeling much better, as she had noticeably perked up when the news about the Roosevelt Hotel came through. At least it would have a bathroom. I bought quantities of flowers for Mrs Newsvendor and expressed our gratitude – genuinely, for it was very kind of them, and the whole disaster was 'just one of those things' – collected the luggage with the help of the taxi-driver, and left a note for Mr Finkelbaum. I have a vague recollection that I saw him again, but I cannot remember where, and there was no unpleasantness about our parting. I felt that I ought to have paid for his petrol, but I thought that he might be insulted, as he had already reluctantly allowed me to pay for our inexpensive tea.

The Roosevelt was bliss after our previous experience, and we even contrived to throw a party in the kitchen after a wonderful visit to the Washington equivalent of our National Gallery. I had to pay for this accommodation, but, as one always does, I had brought with me much more money than could possibly be necessary, and we survived.

After Washington, we had a very enjoyable and restful holiday. No one could call Washington in all that heat, restful, even if things had fallen out as they should have done.

Harold and Dottie Williams of Richmond, Virginia, were the best of hosts, Harold Russell of Atlanta is a great friend who had been very kind to my step-daughter, Jenny, and we were superbly entertained at Barrington, Illinois when we went to Chicago. Our last host who died shortly afterwards and whose name unfortunately escapes me, was very pleased when the other two house guests, Harry Law and Pat Cotes-Preedy, presented him with the bob-wig of the late Lord du Parcq, suitably fumigated. He tried it on with alacrity, and posed for photographs. He was not young and it was all rather sweet. He used to produce good French wine in the evening with dinner : none of your 'coffee, tea, or milk'. His widow remarried and I hope that she will forgive my lapse of memory in the unlikely event of her ever coming across this book.

Harold Russell who is counsel for Eastern Airlines, an important appointment, came to one of the children's weddings, and when informed that I was now a judge in the Divorce Division, said sagely : 'A soft option.'

CHAPTER SIX

Tommy Steele and Bruce Forsyth

It is a long time since I was involved in litigation concerning Tommy Steele or Bruce Forsyth, but they still top the bill. Indeed I read recently in a newspaper that the former is well on his way to his second million. He must be very well advised, if this is really true, in view of the penal taxation prevailing today, and I am just a little sceptical. Whether they will go down to history as the Cockney and the Scotsman, like Dan Leno and Harry Lauder, I wouldn't like to say, nor whether they will last, or indeed want to last, as long as Jack Hulbert and Dame Cicely Courtneidge, but at the present day they remain household words and I will mention the cases briefly, although they are of no intrinsic interest apart from the personalities involved. I did try once to remind Mr Hulbert of one of my favourite lyrics which ended :

> Will you have red or white?
> Well I'll have both tonight,
> I'm on my alco-holiday.

He denied all knowledge of it. Perhaps it was Jack Buchanan.

The case about Tommy Steele was a libel action which involved the question as to which of two pairs of agents were the rightful managers of this desirable discovery, a twenty-two year old genius, serving at that time in the Merchant Navy. The principal witness was to be Mr Steele's forty-three year old mother, who might or might not agree with the statements to be put forward on behalf of my clients, who admittedly had discovered him, but had not necessarily put him under contract.

Buster Milmo, who had still not taken silk, was against me and made a forceful opening speech. When it came to cross-examining the plaintiffs, matters were not too difficult, for they had said in their propaganda that their 'prize' earned more in a month than did the Prime Minister in a year. As they received 40% gross of the star's earnings, (that is, less 10% to booking agents, travelling, advertising, publicity, entertainment, and other outgoings needed to keep him in the public eye), they clearly earned a great deal more than the average juryman trying the case, which would not be very endearing.

But Mrs Steele was another matter. By the time that I had finished cross-examining her – and I had put all I knew into it, for the complications of the case had taken a lot of mastering – it was plain to me that I had not scratched the surface of her credibility. Juries are, as I had learned, unpredictable, but I should have been amazed if I had been able to persuade that jury that Mrs Steele either had a defective recollection or was lying. She was far too impressive a witness for that. And she was the lynch-pin. All the thirty-five witnesses that I had intended to call would not matter if Mrs Steele were to be believed.

So I told my solicitors, who were instructed by an insurance company, that we had better cut our losses and see what terms we could get. They were delighted, for the insurance company had not wanted to fight in the first place, having the truer instinct, although they had readily undertaken to provide the funds once I had said that our people's account might be accepted, in which case they would win. It was at the end of the sixth day of the case that I went to see my opponent with an offer of damages, which was accepted, and a sincere apology. I felt that the enemy had behaved reasonably, and I said so –

> Betwixt the stirrup and the ground,
> Mercy I asked and mercy found

– an expression with which I had been brought up. Next day *The Times* told us that it was Camden's epitaph, whoever he may have been, and set it out differently so that it looks as though I probably misquoted it.

I said: 'In particular, I hope that the lady, whom I have been obliged to accuse of lying, understands that my apology to the Plaintiffs extends also to her.'

For some reason, this ordinary little apology, which would have passed unnoticed if a theatrical personality had not been involved, became an item of news. The late David Jacobs, the solicitor who had acted for the plaintiffs and had procured all the celebrities to support Liberace, sent me a greetings telegram all the way from Whitehall to the Temple: 'Thank you for your courtesy and consideration.' And one of the national newspapers quoted Mr Steele, who never had to give evidence (as I had given in), as having murmured (of me), 'He's a real gent. What I call a toff.' Later in the same article, however, I find it easier to discern the ring of truth : 'I travel all this way from Blackpool for a command performance and the audience walk out on me before I can do my stuff. It's the first time it's ever happened to me, mate.' And the *Sunday Dispatch* headed its article on the subject 'An Act of Grace'.

I am, and always have been, a great supporter of the press, and I realised that all this was because they have to some extent to give the public what it wants, and what it wanted at that time was anything that remotely related to Tommy Steele.

With Bruce Forsyth, however, the question was whether he was bound by his agreement with his agent as a term of which he had to pay that gentleman 15% of his very substantial earnings. Mr Justice Melford Stevenson put his finger on the point by saying, 'I have often heard it said that it is more difficult to get rid of an agent than a wife.' (Laughter in court in which his Lordship joined.)

After a day or two of battle I seem to recollect that the matter was ended amicably, and that the agent's agreement which was due to end in May 1963 was extended for another five years. I may be wrong about that, but it is not altogether extraordinary, for in actions between Miss Shirley Bassey and her ex-manager in which each had claimed damages against the other I am recorded as saying that 'the settlement of the actions had brought about so complete a restoration of the previous amicable relationships between the parties, that Miss Bassey had once again appointed Mr Sullivan her personal manager under an agreement recently signed between them.'

It sounds as though the lawyers had done very well as peace-makers, and I am amused to note that it was Mr David Jacobs who was instructing David Hirst and myself on that last occasion.

No doubt it is clear that mine was an unusual practice dealing with all sorts of odd cases, rather than with the normal mixture of crime and industrial accidents. It all depends on your chambers. In my rather exotic chambers it was all very fine if you came off, but, if you did not, you were wise to move. I can think of seven names of barristers who moved away, and, by the time that I went on the Bench at the age of fifty-four, Colin Duncan was the only one who had been there all the time. If you were brilliant enough to get into Essex Court (McNair, Mocatta, Megaw, Roskill, Donaldson, Kerr, McCrindle; it was

Dickinson and Willink and McNair when I started) you were made, and if you were selected for the 'Factory' which housed Soskice, Armstrong-Jones and Platts-Mills as juniors before the war and has since produced, as judges, O'Connor, Eveleigh and Griffiths, you were unlikely to fail.

But I knew nothing of the Factories Acts and indeed found it an interesting new field when I went on to the Bench. I was not very good at it however.

When, therefore, my clerk Lionel came into my room and said that I was to lead in an accident case and that the papers would be coming down that afternoon, I said that I wasn't very good at 'ladders' (half the accident cases are because someone had fallen off a ladder or slipped on an alleged pool of oil).

He put his finger to his mouth and said conspiratorially, 'Oppenheimer's'.

I said, 'That's different.'

Messrs Herbert Oppenheimer, Nathan and Vandyk, had good commercial work, and David Hirst and I had been against them in an incredibly heavy civil commercial fraud case. They had been to Gilbert Paull, and Gilbert had recently become a judge, in the middle of a case in which Sir Lionel Heald and I were against him for Vandervell, the roller-bearing millionaire, a very dear man. There might, I thought, be an opening there, especially as they had already recognised David's ability.

My client was a rich young man who had met with an accident while water-skiing at Monte Carlo. The driver of the motor-boat against whom he brought the action was uninsured. My young man had had to have a leg amputated, and suffered a fractured left knee, cuts, and a broken jaw. He had had a lucrative career open to him as a stockbroker, which was no longer open to him in his wheel-chair. There were many other items calling for damages for pain and suffering, loss of amenities, and of future prospects. His hospital charges alone amounted to £5,236, treatment being given in New York, and it was argued that he ought to have been treated less expensively in France, or to have come here to be treated free at the taxpayers' expense under the National Health Service. He was Canadian born, educated at Oxford, and employed in a stockbroker's office in Montreal. I rather thought that my opponent, now Lord Justice Ormrod, who is an elected Fellow of the Royal College of Physicians and I should think the only High Court Judge who has ever achieved that distinction, must have had his tongue in his cheek when he made that, to me, preposterous submission. Why you and I should have paid for a Canadian's accident in France, I couldn't see. And I still can't.

The Judge would have none of this. He said that it was reasonable for the plaintiff to have what his uncle considered the best possible surgical and medical treatment to be obtained, and that, as he was in any event going back to Canada, it was proper for him to be taken to New York by air, accompanied by a doctor and a nurse, to a hospital to which a specialist who was a personal friend of his uncle was attached. The uncle had given evidence that £1,000 per month was a standard charge, for in a private ward a patient needed three nurses each of whom received £7 per day. 'You must have to pay whacking premiums,' said Mr Justice Streatfeild, when told that most Americans were covered by insurance.

The defence called no evidence and the Judge found, as I had rather shakily argued, for mechanical matters are not my forte, that the wobble of the boat, which threw the plaintiff and two other people into the water, was caused by the gear lever in the forward position being brought back through neutral into reverse while the throttle was open, and that that was not what a reasonably careful driver would do.

The damages were £51,865.6.6 which was at that time a record, and which if one trebles for inflation in the ensuing fourteen years, might possibly still be so.

The uninsured defendant did not appeal, and it transpired that he was a co-heir to a fortune amounting to millions, and the damages and costs were paid in full. I do not recall what I was paid, but if the venue had been in America where the attorney gets a very substantial percentage of the damages if the client wins, and nothing if he loses, Messrs Herbert Oppenheimer, Nathan and Vandyk would have had occasion to throw a party.

CHAPTER SEVEN

A Polish Military Hero

Peter Rawlinson and I took silk on the same day in 1959, he a young man who had been called after the war, and who was entitled to silk as having been a Member of Parliament for a suitable number of years rather than because of the size of his practice. He had done one murder case extremely well, something to do with a tow-path, but was not nationally known. Four years later he was Solicitor-General, and later Attorney-General for a long time, and a stupendous success in both appointments, in the latter remembering always that his job was to be the leader of the Bar, and not merely a grey political figure. The Bar knew, admired and liked him, and I for one will be delighted if he is our next Lord Chancellor.

It was this comparatively young man who took me on in 1960 in the most interesting libel action I have ever fought. I had been called to the Bar in 1930 and had been dealing in defamation for a long, long time, but he was young, extremely handsome with a lilt in his voice, and he knew the facts and, most important of all, he was on the right side.

He was appearing for a military hero and he did the case beautifully. But oh! how I would have loved to have been in his shoes. He had recently gone into Gerald Gardiner's chambers, a healthy sign, for Gardiner was a Pacifist Socialist, and Peter was a Tory. I don't mean anything offensive to Gerald in that, for he drove his ambulance during the war with the best of them and I was delighted when, having spent so much of his life working for the good of others, he was at last made a Companion of Honour. But I believe that there are some chambers of political barristers in the Temple, and that I don't think looks well. So that when Peter went into Gerald's chambers it looked as though profession and politics were being kept apart, which is good.

I have never understood these pacifists myself. I had one great friend to whom I was always pointing out that, whilst I had great respect for his immortal soul, surely we should all be under Hitler's heel if we were all like him or like the late Herbert Morrison. (I used to throw that in because he was a very strong Tory.) He never made much sense in argument. Then one day in 1943 he called in on me in Beirut dressed as a private soldier. I gave him a cup of coffee, and he revealed that he was going to do something as a stretcher-bearer, and 'they' had taken him as he had agreed that, if the foe attacked him, he would fight back. I wished him luck. It then turned out that 'something' meant parachuting into Sardinia, a useless enterprise, because he was apprehended almost immediately and put in the bag. But I hold nothing against that sort of pacifist.

However, I confess that the thought entered my head that Gardiner might have thought that this was not quite his sort of case, and that that was why Peter was here. He led Milmo, of course, and I led Peter Bristow in Milmo's chambers (now Mr Justice Bristow), and Stephen Terrell, in the same chambers, was for a co-defendant. I suspect that the only reason why I was in it was because there was at that time no silk in those chambers, of which dear old Heseltine, the managing clerk with Lewis & Lewis, was a staunch supporter. And Gardiner and I were the only available professionals.

So, in the previous summer I had been sent a brief to advise on evidence jointly with my junior, (which means that money is no object, for the junior can perfectly well do it by himself) and I spent a lot of the Long Vacation in the garden in a deck-chair under a weeping hornbeam thinking how hopeless the case was and thanking heaven that at least the plaintiff had written a book which I learned almost by heart. 'Mine enemy has written a book' is a tag all barristers know, for it is always possible to find material for cross-examination in the opponent's brainchild.

The plaintiff was the great General Vladyslaw Anders whom King George VI had made a Companion of the Bath after the Poles under his command had taken Monte Cassino with the loss of 281 officers and 3,500 men out of a force of 17,000, who had been wounded eight times in battle, who had been awarded the Legion d'Honneur and the Croix de Guerre, who had gained the highest Polish decoration, the Virtute Militari, four times, who had commanded his regiment in the field under Marshal Pilsudski in the Polish-Soviet war from 1919 to 1922 and fought against the Germans in 1939 until captured by the Russians and imprisoned in the dreaded Lubianka prison, who had led the Polish army out of Russia into Persia and to the Middle East, who had commanded the second Polish Corps throughout the Italian Campaign, and

who had been appointed Commander in Chief of the Polish Army in
1945.

I remembered the poor Poles in their tattered greatcoats staring dejectedly at the snow in Campobasso, in 1944, looking as though they
could do with a good square meal. They had been in my mind for
many years. I had thought of them again in 1945, when I saw the
wretched Chetniks who had served under Mihailovich standing in
desperate groups by the side of the road near Trieste, waiting to be
massacred.

I had thought of them again later in 1945 when I was in Graz, and
heard of the fate of the Ukrainians whom we had agreed at Yalta to
turn over to the Russians and to death. The language barrier is really
a dreadful thing. If only we had all spoken Esperanto at Campobasso
we could have made those Poles less miserable, I am sure. Some of
them looked very old.

So this was the man I was to cross examine if ever the case was fought.
What had we said about him?

> The Association of Polish Generals insists that General Anders
> should be proclaimed president or 'leader of fighting Poland' – he
> who during World War I did not yet consider himself a Pole and
> refused to take part in the battle of Warsaw, and who during World
> War II was against Sikorski's government and believed in Hitler's
> victory . . . Adam Gas.

My Mr Gas, who had written this letter, lived in London and was
working as a machine operator on night shift at the time, while the
other defendant, Mr Kwiatowski, owned a Polish-language newspaper
printed in France, where he lived, and where there were a great many
Polish miners. The newspaper only had a circulation of about 300
copies a day in England.

The General complained of the words : —

(1) 'who during World War I did not yet consider himself a Pole';
(2) 'who refused to take part in the Battle of Warsaw' (there were
    battles of Warsaw in 1920 and 1939);
(3) 'who during World War II was against Sikorski's government';
(4) 'who believed in Hitler's victory'.

I wasn't surprised that he did complain. I wrote a long advice on
evidence, never thinking that the case would ever come to trial, and
sent back the book, *An Army in Exile*, with the papers, to Messrs Lewis
& Lewis. In the past, I had walked from June Farm to Leigh (pro-

nounced 'Lie') and round through Betchworth back to home, perfecting a cross-examination of Miss Vivien Leigh (pronounced 'Lee'), who was cross about something, only to find that the case was settled. But now I was older, and I was sure that this hopeless action could not be contested.

Not at all: it was a political battle and it could not be settled. The mining community at Lens were anti-Anders to a man, and reports of the trial, and particularly of my cross-examination of the General, would step up circulation enormously, and to apologise to him would involve a loss of face which could not be tolerated.

It was all very sad. Both parties hated the Communists, the Russians. The General had come out of prison in Moscow weighing eight stone and on crutches. Before his incarceration he had weighed fourteen stone. He was an inflexible enemy of Russia.

My people were the Polish Peasant Party, led by Mr Mikolajczyk, who had been a member of General Sikorski's government in exile and was made Deputy Prime Minister to General Sikorski and Minister of the Interior in 1943.

They were all very heroic in their different ways. My Mr Gas, who obviously had let his pen run away with him, had fought the Germans in 1939, was attacked from the back by the Russians, escaped to Silesia, joined the underground movement and was caught by the Gestapo in 1941, escaped, and was sentenced to death for high treason in his absence. Two more years underground, and he was arrested and sent to Auschwitz. He showed the jury the mark on his left arm. Number 125,604. Then the Russians took him from Auschwitz in 1945 and put him in a concentration camp in Austria. There the Americans liberated him, and he came to England in 1946. Before the war the poor fellow had led a blameless life in Poland as a school-teacher and secretary of a Protestant youth movement.

His fellow defendant, Mr Kwiatowski, for his part, had been condemned to death by the German High Command during the War for his activities, and was a member of the Christian Catholic Party. He was seventy-seven and had been running a newspaper since 1909. It was a dreadful thing that these differences between Polish emigrés should be debated with such violence in court, and I said to the jury how sad it was, because, whatever happened, the principal beneficiary would be the Communist Government in Warsaw, whom both factions hated.

My side's case was that General Anders and the whole military junta were enemies of Sikorski's government. As Mr Mikolajczyk put it, 'The foreign policy of Sikorski's government was to fight the Germans and sway the country by the activities of the underground. In the end, there were 300,000 fighters in the underground. It was also part of the policy always to be in good relations with other countries, including Soviet Russia. The presence of the Polish Army in Russia was necessary as a protection for the whole of the Polish population spread throughout Russia. It was wrong for Anders to agree with Stalin that the Polish army should be evacuated from Russia. The Sikorski government had never agreed to it. If the Poles had been driven out by Stalin, then they should have come back from Persia to fight on Russian soil, and have entered Poland again from the East. As soon as the Army had been evacuated from Russia, the Russians liquidated completely the social welfare side of the embassy and declared that the Poles in Russia were now Russian citizens. They accused the Poles of running away and said that they didn't want to fight Hitler.'

Anders, on the other hand, said that Sikorski himself had prepared the transfer of the whole Army to the Middle East as the Russians had not carried out the terms of the amnesty, and he produced the minutes of a meeting on 3rd December 1941 between Stalin, Molotov, Ambassador Kot, General Sikorski and himself when Stalin was reported as saying (in a tone of irritation and annoyance), 'I am an experienced old man. I do know that once you leave for Persia you will never return. I can see that England has a lot of work to do and needs Polish soldiers. . . . If you are set on it, one corps, two or three divisions, can go. I have received demands from Churchill and Roosevelt for the evacuation of the Polish Army.'

We called a great number of witnesses, some very distinguished. Professor Stanislaw Kot, who was Polish Ambassador to Moscow in 1941, said that Sikorski had sent a telegram to Anders that for reasons of high policy the troops had to stay in Soviet Russia. He also had written a book. He said that Stalin's headquarters had promised Sikorski a great strong Polish Army to fight alongside the Soviets when they entered Poland in due course. Later Stalin had had some success against the Germans and wanted to get rid of the Poles, and used Anders as his cover to fulfil his wish. This old gentleman also produced a bizarre theory about General Sikorski having been murdered. His idea was not that put forward in Hochhuth's *The Soldiers* (against which, to my delight, a jury in this country awarded £50,000 libel damages), namely that Sir Winston Churchill contrived the General's death, but there was a vague cloak and dagger atmosphere. He stated that he knew

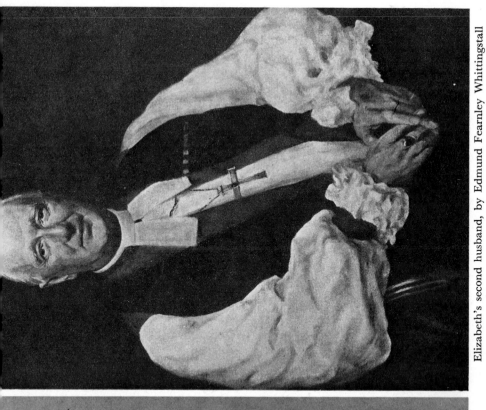

Elizabeth's second husband, by Edmund Fearnley Whittingstall

Major Tristram Kirkwood RE, Elizabeth's first husband

Elizabeth and Number Three, May 27, 1967
'Do you really love me'

that there were people in the Army in the Middle East who plotted for the General's last journey and death, but he didn't know to what extent the Germans caused it, or who was the tool of the Germans in Gibraltar.

In cross-examination he agreed that an adjutant of General Anders, a Captain Klimkowski, who was subsequently court-martialled and sentenced, had written a book in which he had accused Sir Winston and General Anders for being responsible for Sikorski's death. He added that that was why he refused to have anything to do with this unreliable person when he came to this country. (Whether Mr Hochhuth knew all about this, I cannot say.)

Count Adam Romer, Secretary-General to the Polish government under General Sikorski and under Mr Mikolajczyk, said that Sikorski's view was that any breach with Russia would be a sentence of death for many thousands of civilians, some of whom were the next of kin to the Polish soldiers. He said that Anders was disloyal.

Madame Sikorski, the widow, and a Mr Popill also spoke against the plaintiff.

So we had some ammunition on the political issue although it seemed to me painfully obvious that Anders had taken the right decision to get as many people as possible out of Russia while he could. If Sikorski's plan had been followed and they had all stopped there, I am sure that once the Russians had finished with Hitler, the Poles would have been liquidated.

I do not know for how many days I cross-examined this very distinguished soldier. I certainly spent the best part of a day cross-examining him, with the assistance of an enormous map pinned to a wall of the court, concerning the part that he had played in the Battle of Warsaw 1939. It wasn't easy, as the cross-examination was all based on a book which a Colonel Schweizer had written. He had apparently been relieved of his command by General Anders and felt very angry about it, and eventually when he, rather unexpectedly, appeared to give evidence, it was a question of whom the jury believed.

Eventually I managed to get the General to agree that in 1943 he thought it was best to get rid of Sikorski's government and have a 'strong' government instead. He conceded that he knew that his proposal to evacuate Poles to the Middle East was unacceptable to Sikorski. If that didn't show that he was an enemy of Sikorski's government, I couldn't think what did.

I think that I summarised it fairly when I said to the jury that the key to the whole question, could be found in a few sentences of two letters passing between the Generals. Anders wrote : 'It is quite clear to us that the Soviets have deceived us, and this must be proclaimed everywhere. It must be confirmed by a very strong statement addressed to the world and to Poland.' In answer, General Sikorski said : 'A breach with Russia would be a sentence of death for hundreds of thousands of next of kin of our soldiers who still remain there.'

Numerous generals gave evidence on either side. They all seemed to have written books, except an English general who appeared for the plaintiff but conceded that he only spoke six words of Polish, which rather handicapped him. A former Polish Ambassador gave evidence for General Anders, as did the one time head of the Polish Military Mission to Moscow, General Bogusz-Szysko, and a number of others. I persuaded the ex-Ambassador to say that Churchill's *The Second World War* was absolutely wrong as to Poland, which I thought might help with the jury. I managed to parry most of the witnesses adequately, because they were all so proud of their English that they wouldn't have an interpreter. Madness, of course. (Always get your client to give evidence through an interpreter; then he is virtually untouchable. I think of Lord Rank who disdained his deaf aid in a case I described in *No Mitigating Circumstances*.)

Poor old Anders, with whom I got on very well, was a gentleman and he trusted me. When there was an objection, he said, 'Yes. We are having a very interesting discussion.' When there was another objection, *The Times* records the Judge as saying, 'I have never in my lifetime heard a cross-examination conducted with such exemplary fairness with a witness of whom advantage might be taken.'

I assumed then that they would put that on my tombstone. However, today I think a cremation is cleaner and we don't want to clutter up our overcrowded island with graves.

Anders would have done better with an interpreter but it would have made the case last much longer and have cost my clients more in the long run.

One point that amused me and has always baffled me was when, in re-examination, Peter Rawlinson referred to a message from Professor Kot of 27th October 1942 in which he said that 'General Anders endeavours to suppress all improper behaviour, such as accosting women in the camp, or making improper jokes about the English in stage performances.' I so much regret that in all the astonishing detail of the case, I neglected to ascertain what exactly were these improper jokes which the plaintiff calvinistically suppressed.

Generals, Prime Ministers, Ambassadors, Cabinet Secretaries, Foreign Ministers and so on may not have cut much ice with an English jury. After all, they were emigrés quarrelling among themselves and, unless there were jurors who had served in the war, it would not mean a lot to them.

But my opponent had a rod in pickle for me. After the plaintiff's long stay in the witness box, when I don't know which of the two of us was the more exhausted, Peter casually announced that he would now call Field Marshal Earl Alexander of Tunis.

Oh dear! What was I to do? The ex-Minister of Defence was obviously, and surprisingly, extremely nervous. He merely said that General Anders was a splendid character who was devoted to the Allied cause, and that the Poles did extremely well at Cassino. So I got up and said, 'I only rise to cross-examine so that I can tell my grand-children that I once cross-examined a Field Marshal.' I then made some trumpery point about Cassino, near to which I had been at Presenzano in my non-combatant role, and sat down with relief.

As you can imagine, all this uphill battle was very hard work.

In the same manner as we had produced an unexpected colonel to support our evidence of the Battle of Warsaw in 1939, we, incredibly, flew over a gentleman, who would now be over eighty, from Pennsylvania, to tell the jury that the plaintiff in December 1915 had said that he was not a Pole, and that he would have the witness court-martialled if he ever spoke Polish.

As to the alleged belief in Hitler's victory, General Anders said that he had often stated that he feared that Hitler would go through the Caucasus. Indeed he had told Mr Churchill so, and General Alan-brooke had agreed with him. But he had never said that Germany would beat Russia, although, if Hitler had not made mistakes, he might well have done.

So at the end of the day, I thought that I had shown that the General was an enemy of Sikorski's government, but that the other matters depended on whether the jury believed the General on the one hand, or Professor Kot and the character from Pennsylvania and the dis-gruntled Colonel on the other. I knew whom I believed but I had to persuade the jury to the contrary.

Of course I failed, even though vanity has caused me to preserve a note passed up to me by old Heseltine, praise from whom was praise indeed. It reads: 'Congratulations on your wonderful – forceful – and (I hope) convincing speech. E.G.H.'

The jury did find that it was true to say that the General had been an enemy of Sikorski's government during the War, and also very sensibly found that it was not defamatory to say so. For the rest, this great man's reputation was vindicated, and the jury fixed the damages at £7,000.

It had been a scrupulously fair summing up. In dealing with the meaning of that awful word 'malice', which has caused us so much trouble in the Committee on Defamation, to which I shall refer later, the Judge took a sensible and novel approach which was, if anything, to the defendant's advantage and did not really square with the official definition of 'any indirect motive'. He referred the jury to the Litany which spoke of 'envy, hatred, malice, and all uncharitableness', and said that that gave one clue as to what the law meant. He continued, and I only quote him out of vanity, that in some cases the conduct of the defence at the trial might be evidence of malice, but that in the present case the jury should put it right out of their minds. For it was a matter for which the jury and he should be grateful, that with such grave charges, counsel for the defendant was able to conduct his case with the restraint he had shown.

What ho! !

The late Mr Justice Ashworth concluded by saying that General Anders was probably the best known living Pole and that it was an important case. If the jury found in his favour he was entitled to reasonable, not small damages. This was an exceptionally distinguished Judge, and the jury did as he wished.

We argued about costs and the General was given only two-thirds of the costs of the action. That I thought to be correct as at least one third of the time had been taken up with the issue on which he failed, and on which he was foolish to have relied, when he was almost certain to win on the other three points.

I have expressed my opinion often enough in other places that it is wrong that one party to a defamation action should be able to force a jury on the other against his will. The mode of trial should be decided by an independent legal functionary such as a Master of the Supreme Court, with an Appeal to a Judge in chambers, and from him to the Court of Appeal. Compare the small sums awarded to Miss Tracy (£3,000) and to Mr Waugh (£2,000) with those given to Mr Patino* and to Lord Keyes and – we shall shortly come to him – to Mr Lewis

---

*See *No Mitigating Circumstances*, pp. 146, 168, 180.

with his £217,000, and it can be seen that the present situation is most unsatisfactory.

Judges, sitting alone, are not so generous when putting their hands into other people's pockets. But if ever there was a case in favour of juries this was the one. The subject matter rendered it suitable for a jury (and no doubt a Master would have so ordered), they answered all the questions correctly, and they fixed a reasonable figure for damages.

I think I served my clients well in that case in difficult circumstances, and it is the case in my career to which I look back with most satisfaction.

CHAPTER EIGHT

The Sound of Music

General Anders' case was heard in February, 1960, and Tommy Steele and Bruce Forsyth and indeed Mr Finkelbaum, all of whom came later, have been put in out of order for the purpose of avoiding cramming the heavy cases one on top of the other which might not annoy the lawyer, but would be indigestible for the layman.

I had been in court for months without a break, and had had to cope with the Jasper report as well. Thus it was a very tired man of fifty-two, feeling like seventy-two, who was picked up at 1 Brick Court on a Friday evening during the Anders case, to be driven to Oxford by a couple of undergraduates in one of the smallest and most uncomfortable cars I have ever seen.

Many months before, when I had not begun to be madly busy, I had been asked to propose the toast of the immortal memory of Blackstone at Pembroke College, Oxford, of which he was presumably an alumnus. It appeared that they had combed the hedges for speakers, starting at Norman Birkett and working downwards, until they ended up with me. I was in a very weak position, for the secretary of the College Law Society was the son of Stuart Coulson, a very old friend of mine who had helped me keep the wolf from the door by sending me work in my early years, and had been put in the bag at Saint Valery-en-Caux and had spent five years as a POW. It was obviously my duty to help him out. I put up a brave fight by pointing out that I might be in court on the day in question, in which case there was no train to Oxford which would get me there in time.

When, however, I was told I should be fetched by car I gave in peacefully. So there we were bowling along that hellish road to High Wycombe on a cold February evening, where I was unable even to stretch my legs, and wanted nothing more than to do so, have a nap, and a glass of whisky when I woke up. We conversed politely and more or less endlessly, so that there was no chance of thinking about the

Immortal Memory. I had not done my homework properly, for during the past weeks I had eaten, drunk and slept Anders and nothing but Anders. I knew that Blackstone had written the famous *Commentaries*, which I had never read, and that the Americans were much more worked up about them than we were. (The poor fellow died in 1780 at the age of only fifty-seven.) Silks don't take pupils, and the only person I could have sent to do some research and prepare some urbane and witty comments on the author's private life and that sort of thing was David Hirst, who was much too valuable, holding my hand in court and seeing that I did not make too many facetious remarks, to be spared for such a chore. Had I gone to Oxford by train in an empty carriage I might have thought of something to say, but trying to do so in a little car, while carrying on a conversation simultaneously, only produced a splitting headache.

The driver was very competent and we duly arrived at Oxford, where I was shown to a guest room which might have been designed for Edward the Confessor. I performed my ablutions to the best of my ability, donned my dinner jacket, and went to meet my fate. I imagine that the undergraduates had to pay for my meal and that of the other guests, so that it was only natural that I should be offered a glass of sherry, which did nothing for my headache, rather than a large whisky and water which might have had its effect. The great Professor Heuston was there, then editor of *Salmond on Torts* and finishing his *Lives of the Lord Chancellors*. He engaged me in interesting legal 'shop', and we went into dinner.

My old friend's son, who was due to say a few words to introduce me, was on my right and we carried on a desultory conversation, for we were both fairly drained after the journey from the Temple. I thought he was looking rather pale but did not take it seriously as I didn't know him well. When his turn came however, he got to his feet, said one sentence, and fell heavily down on the floor in a faint, and was carried out of the room unconscious.

This was rather alarming, but gave me the chance to say that clearly I was not the only nervous person in the room that evening, and I was sure that they would understand if my speech was short rather than long. I gave them about ten minutes only about half of which, I fear, was devoted to Blackstone, and received polite rather than enthusiastic applause. It had been my worst post-prandial effort and I have made hundreds of after dinner speeches. Fortunately the day was saved by a visitor, a Fellow of Worcester College, who after saying that it was a pity that the speaker hadn't been able to tell them anything about Blackstone, did not fill the gap himself, but electrified his audience with some observations about a bridge at Oxford with which he apparently had some connection – remarks too parochial for me, but clearly very much to some point or other.

Then to what at Cambridge would have been the JCR, for many conversations largely with overseas students who were bursting to talk shop. Eventually, still with my headache, and not reluctantly, to bed. Back to June Farm from Oxford by train; most of Saturday gone. Why in the world we do these things, I often wonder. I imagine that it is a sense of duty, and no doubt I should have enjoyed it if I had not been so tired and had had time to prepare my brief. As it was, I felt rather ashamed to have let my host down, and could only derive some consolation from the fact that, while I was doing so, he was unconscious.

My dear friend Harry Phillimore went to the Probate, Divorce and Admiralty Division whence he was transferred to the Queen's Bench Division. I only appeared before him once, on behalf of a heavy-weight but highly respected impresario called Henry Sherek, who had put on a play called *It's in the Bag*. The *Daily Express* published a review headed 'This play should not have got out of its bag', which I thought amusing and possibly fair comment, although I had not read the play. However, a writ was issued and Milmo and I were tee'd up for a great battle when the matter was compromised. I was instructed on behalf of the plaintiff to make one of the most half-witted statements of all time : 'The defendants were appearing today by counsel in order to make it clear that the observations to which the plaintiff had taken objection were never intended to be understood in a *literal* (!) sense and to express to the plaintiff their sincere regret that this was not made clear to their readers and to withdraw it unreservedly.' Buster Milmo had to waffle away about 'the contribution to the theatrical life of the country by the plaintiff's productions over the years.'

I didn't ask; but to me it smelt like 'no damages, no costs'. And the record was withdrawn, and everyone was satisfied.

Immediately after Geoffrey Lawrence had defeated me in the Court of Appeal in the case where the amount of the payment in had been disclosed, I found myself, with two juniors, fighting the Solicitor-General also with two juniors, one of whom is now Lord Justice Cumming-Bruce and the other Judge Barr. The case involved a very large sum of money received by the Commissioners of Customs and Excise from Grundig (Great Britain) Ltd, for whom I had a very soft spot as I had recorded my Jasper report on one of their instruments. The company, for whom I appeared, had paid a large amount of import duty on tape recorders under protest, and they sought to recover it.

There were two actions. In the first, we said that our Stenorette machines were 'machines of the type used for recording dictated correspondence'. If so, 10% duty was payable. The Government said on the other hand that they were 'combined recorders and reproducers (complete with amplifiers) for magnetic sound recording on tape or wire' and thus subject to 20%.

In the second action, brought after the Government had altered the orders, the question was : 'Could the machines properly be described as dictating machines?' and if so 'were they suitable for the recording or reproduction of music?'

All this sounds extremely boring, but it was nothing of the kind.

I was instructed to bring the question of music into the forefront of the attack, with the object of showing that the machines were not suitable for the recording or reproducing of music. I suggested that we might call Professor Andrade as a witness. Professor Edward Neville da Costa Andrade was a most distinguished man and an experienced expert witness. He knew about everything scientific and was an expert on such divergent subjects as claret and music. I knew that Guy Aldous had had him several times as a witness in patent actions and that his opinion had found favour with the court. And I had appeared for him in an arbitration when he was Director in the Royal Institution and a faction wanted to get him out. I called Sir Henry Dale, Lord Halsbury, Lord Falmouth, Sir Thomas Merton and all sorts of people – he was rather upset because Sir Edward Appleton at the last moment couldn't come. Eventually, the Royal Institution gave in on agreed terms, which were ultimately breached on the grounds that it was 'only a gentleman's agreement'. David (lately Lord Justice) Cairns was against me in the case, and felt as strongly as I did about the breach of faith. The villain of the piece, I am sorry to say, was a Queen's Counsel, now deceased, whom I do not name.

The Professor went into bat with his head held high and was very grand indeed. He had however clearly neglected to observe that the late Mr Justice Barry, the most delightful of men, didn't know a trombone from a tuba, and was obviously worried about the musical issue, which I had been ill-advised to prefer. When, in answer to the Solicitor-

General, Percy Andrade agreed that the machines recorded music, but did not faithfully record music, although 'if it were Tommy Steele, I should not think that it would make much difference', it was clear to me that this approach was doomed.

When I heard the Solicitor-General muttering to himself, as he rushed off to luncheon, 'Well, if I can't win this case, I can't win anything' my views were confirmed. My solicitor, however, was made of sterner stuff, and the late Mr Eric Robinson, a nationally known figure on the BBC of whom the Judge would certainly have heard, was produced in the twinkling of an eye. He did splendidly, but in the end the Solicitor-General reduced him to agreeing that, while he did not think that any-one with a sense of musical appreciation would purchase an unadapted tape recorder, a housewife who wanted music while washing up might not mind the standard of reproduction.

That ended the third day, and clearly we had to start serving into the backhand court. We must show that these were 'dictating machines' bought and sold as such, and the fact that they could be used for recording and reproducing music was irrelevant. My solicitor, Mr R. C. de M. Blum, produced about a dozen witnesses the next day who gave the appropriate evidence. How he got them in so short a time I didn't know. But the euphoria on the Government side seemed to evaporate at first slowly, and then more obviously. We had come up from love forty to deuce.

The Solicitor-General made his very persuasive final speech on Friday : it was much longer than I had hoped, and I had the embarrass-ment of telling Mr Blum, who had marked my brief with four figures, that I couldn't be there on the Monday morning, for I was bound to open the case for the plaintiffs in the very next Court.

He took it very well and allowed Mr Leon Maclaren, whom I haven't seen since the case, to make the final speech instead of me. He did so : it was brilliant as I know, because I read the transcript, and we won. (The solicitors in the other case on Monday morning were not pleased with my performance.)

The Government appealed. Again the Solicitor-General (now Lord Simon of Glaisdale), who is years younger than I am, but nevertheless was a Squadron Sergeant-Major in the Inns of Court Regiment before the war when I was Trooper Faulks, made a splendid speech. All was going swimmingly for him when he mispronounced the word 'bohea'.

Lord Justice Harman, who had looked very bored up to then, but who was Gigadibs the Literary Man, pulled him up at once, 'Bo-hay, surely, Sir Jocelyn', and time was played out on that note. A fevered consultation brought the recommendation from the Secretary of Grundig's, who was as bright as a button (Mr Springer, I think, but I suspect that it wasn't his real name), that I should concentrate on a propaganda document of ours which the Solicitor-General had put in when he was dealing with 'music', which emphasised the dictatory qualities of the machine, its other properties being merely ancillary.

I did a little homework too. On Monday morning I found a very ready audience when I quoted their Lordships a chunk from Pope's 'Rape of the Lock' about 'bohea' and, apart from Harman grunting 'a bit late to introduce this', the pamphlet was a trump card, and the Ship of State was sunk in the absence of the Solicitor-General on public business. Lord Justice Ormerod confessed that during the argument his mind had wavered but . . . etc., etc.

Lord Justice Ormerod was known affectionately as 'Big Ben' for he was about ten feet high and is not to be confused with the present Lord Justice Ormrod who is only about 6ft. 1in. He was originally a County Court Judge in the North Country, and has only just left us. It is remarkable how lawyers live on, and we can take cheer from the fact that Lord Justice Slesser whom no one has seen to my knowledge since 1939 has just passed his ninety-fifth birthday. He has beaten Papa but not my godfather and Uncle Sydney who was ninety-eight on 11th January 1978.

Big Ben was president of the Bar Musical Society and well known to be adept at the piano. I had a case when I was in silk concerning Lloyd's underwriters, which went on and on and on. I started with Lord Scarman, as he now is, against me. He made an impertinent application for an injunction against my clients which for some reason found favour with the Judge in Chambers and with the Court of Appeal. The power of his personality, I suppose. When the case itself came on, we won, and the only question remaining was as to how much damages we should be paid to compensate us for having had to suffer an injunction which had been wrongly granted. During this period, Leslie Scarman had become a judge, and the enemy enlisted the present Mr Justice Arnold. We were awarded a lot of money by Mr Justice Mocatta, after having heard practically every insurance agent in Belgium giving evidence through an interpreter. I had had to leave the last part of the proceedings to David Hirst (who no doubt did better than I should have done, for I was beginning to get bored, and he wasn't) as I had to go to start the great case of *Rookes* v *Barnard*.

However, I was back again in time to conduct the insurance case in the Court of Appeal, where a new opponent emerged in the shape of Mr Eustace (now Lord Justice) Roskill QC. It was primarily a commercial matter, which was his speciality, with overtones of fraud, which was mine. Lord Justice Devlin, as he then was, was one member of the court, so that I didn't have to bother about the commercial aspect, and as to the fraud, it was an appeal from Mr Justice Pearson who was renowned for common sense. Accordingly, I sat quietly waiting for victory.

They called upon me, largely, I think, as a compliment to Eustace who had a very difficult case to argue and at one stage I found myself saying that the vital word in the contract was 'until'.

'Until', interjected Big Ben, 'yes, that word brings back memories to me.'

And I could in my mind's eye see him banging away at the piano while someone in a white tie declaimed a drawing-room ballad. I had gone through it all in my childhood. I decided to risk it.

'No rose in all the world until you came, perhaps, my Lord?'

'Yes, indeed,' he said, and I went on with my argument. When I sat down, Eustace got up to reply and made much about 'Your Lordship's rose,' but I doubted if he really knew what Big Ben and I were talking about.

The Solicitor-General of whom I have been writing was, as I have said, the present Lord Simon of Glaisdale, a literary man apart from being a very good judge. The two do not often go together, and he is an exception, as anyone who had read his articles in the *Law Quarterly Review* or his speeches in the Lords about Race Relations will bear out. I am also indebted to him for his exertions in the House of Lords with regard to The Rehabilitation of Offenders Act much of the draft of which did not appeal to me.

Lord Darling was a literary man who was not generally thought to be a good judge. I can think of a number of very good judges who are not literary men, and would not be pleased to be so-called. All this made the blunder about 'bohea' the more entertaining to me, and I am sure that I am causing no offence in reciting it.

What did rather tickle me was that a few years later, when Jack Simon was the President of the Probate, Divorce and Admiralty Division at it was then called, and I was one of his junior Judges, we had a little conversation. Mind you, this Grundig case was the only one in which we had been opposed to each other. Before he became a politician he had been a divorce specialist; before I took silk, I did very little contested divorce.

I had had an attack of gout and had had to be carted into court in a wheel-chair with everyone pretending to be very deferential, and inwardly roaring with laughter. I had said that I would go and see the premises at Brighton where certain dark deeds were said to have taken place. The solicitors for the husband rang me in the early morning to say that they had compromised the exceedingly disgusting case and I needn't go to Brighton. So I stayed in bed. Having a troublesome conscience I felt impelled to go and tell the 'boss' that I had had a day off, on full pay, with gout. I was hobbling at the time and he said, 'Gout, my dear Neville, I never knew of it. No wonder you were such a formidable adversary when you were at the Bar.'

He meant it so kindly and I don't think that he knew that he had let the cat out of the bag, but when you come to think of it, he could not have been saying anything except, 'You were a bad-tempered old brute to be against.'

While I was doing the Grundig case, my clerk came to me and said that Mr Sebag Shaw wanted to see me after court about something personal. I said, 'Of course', as he was a very old friend who had succeeded me in my job with the Board of Trade at the Old Bailey. He is now, it seems almost unnecessary to say, a highly esteemed Lord Justice, one of our leading criminal experts. He was very worried because he thought that a client, for whom he had appeared in an action for damages for false imprisonment and assault against the police, had not received justice.

It seemed that the issue at the trial was whether the poor little press photographer, who was appropriately named Meek, or the police officer, who was the defendant, and was called Fleming, was telling the truth with regard to a struggle between them in Cannon Row police station when no one else was there.

Each had accused the other of starting the fracas. The plaintiff had been arrested on Guy Fawkes Night, 1958, during a riot in Trafalgar Square of which he was taking photographs. At the time Mr Fleming was a Chief Inspector and was sued as such. Unbeknown to Mr Meek and his advisers, Mr Fleming had got into trouble over a very minor offence which, however, involved his being party to an untruth, as a result of which on 16th December 1959, he was reduced in rank from chief inspector to station sergeant.

This matter had not been mentioned to the Judge or to the jury at the trial, and Sebag Shaw felt that the weight attaching to the word of a chief inspector might have swung the case against his client in a way which might not have occurred if the word of a station sergeant, who had been reduced to that rank by reason of some minor misdemeanour, had been the criterion.

I had to agree with him, having the strong views about the unpredictability of juries which I possess. Station Sergeant Fleming had appeared at the trial and given evidence in plain clothes whereas six or seven other police officers had given evidence in uniform.

During the summing up the Judge had innocently referred to Sergeant Fleming on two occasions as 'Chief Inspector', on seventeen as 'Inspector' and on twenty-three as 'Mr'.

In cross-examination Sergeant Fleming had been asked, 'You are a Chief Inspector and have been in the force since 1938 ?'

His answer was, 'Yes, that is true.' (Note the word 'are'.)

There was a smell. I think that the reason that Sebag came to me was because there was some rather nasty decided law to be got over before we could get a new trial, and not because he didn't want to have to attack his opponent, who was an old friend. If it had been that, he would have gone elsewhere for help, because his opponent was an old friend of mine also, as he knew.

The nasty piece of law was that never had a new trial been granted on the basis of admitting fresh evidence as to credit only, and the House of Lords had said that if you want to set aside a judgment on the ground of fraud the proper thing was not to go to the Court of Appeal but to start a fresh action.

I told Sebag that I thought it our duty to try to see justice done, and we agreed that we would do so without a fee. The way I approached the case was that the defence of Sergeant Fleming, which was supported by the taxpayer indirectly, as it was the solicitor for the Metropolitan Police who appeared for him, was not fraudulent. I said that his advisers, no doubt very carefully and with anxiety, considered their position before the case and decided that in the interests of their client, there was no obligation upon them to tell Mr Meek about the demotion. I said that that was quite wrong, and that they should have considered the interests of justice, of the jury, of the public, and of Mr Meek, as well as that of Sergeant Fleming.

There was no doubt that the evidence of the demotion would normally have had an impact upon the jury, for, as Lord Justice Pearce observed during the argument, 'the clearest evidence that it would have had an impact is the trouble that was taken to conceal it'. It was all very difficult for my unfortunate opponent, who manfully took upon himself all the responsibility, disdaining to suggest that his junior or the solicitor did other than follow his instructions. He said that his decision not to advertise Sergeant Fleming in his reduced rank came from his understanding of counsel's duties set out in a book on *Conduct and Etiquette at the Bar* by Sir William Boulton, who may be remembered from the Finkelbaum episode. He had written :

Any deception of the court must be avoided, but counsel is under no duty to disclose facts known to him regarding his client's character or antecedents, nor to correct any information which may be given to the court by the prosecution, if a correction would be to the client's detriment.

I am sure, writing many years afterwards, that this was just a dreadful mistake of judgement for which, in my view, my poor friend has had to suffer too much. But, with hindsight, it is obvious that the court would be deceived, as is evidenced by the reference to 'Chief Inspector' by the Judge, by the shorthand recording 'copy of extract from Chief Inspector's notebook handed to the jury', and by Sebag and the Judge addressing him on seven occasions as 'Chief Inspector' without correction either by the witness or by counsel.

Having dodged the issue of fraud which might have meant a fresh action instead of going to the Court of Appeal, I decided to do the obvious thing – tell them that the case involved breaking new ground but that it would be more convenient for them if I outlined the facts before coming to the law. By the time I had done that, they were breast high with me, and, mercifully, in browsing through the White Book (the *Annual Practice*, the lawyer's vade mecum) I had discovered a somewhat general observation by the late Viscount Buckmaster as long ago as 1918 in a case improbably entitled *Hip Foong Hong* v *H. Neotia & Company* as follows : 'In all applications for a new trial the fundamental ground must be that there has been a miscarriage of justice.'

It was a simple step from that to propound that, provided that you could show a prima facie case that there had been a miscarriage of justice, you were entitled to a new trial even if it were on the basis of admitting new evidence as to credit only.

Their Lordships agreed and a little bit of new law was made. They

expressed themselves forcibly in their judgments and ordered Sergeant
Fleming to pay the costs of the action and of the appeal. They ordered
a new trial. There never was one, because an offer of damages was made
which Mr Meek accepted.

I imagine that the taxpayer paid for it all, for Sergeant Fleming could
say that he only did as he was told by his advisers.

The case has not affected my friendship with my opponent which I
consider extremely generous of him, for I had to say a number of unkind things, however heavily I tried to disguise them. A national newspaper decided to tell the world that I had done the case without fee
which 'provided an example of the Bar's high tradition'. So that didn't
do me any harm, and two dozen bottles of the most excellent hock
appeared, ostensibly from my client. As I was quite sure that they really
came from my solicitor, my client being by no means well to do, I
decided after much thought not to treat them as a fee for tax purposes
but as an unsolicited gift from 'an admirer'. If this book comes to the
attention of the Revenue and I was wrong, I am prepared to pay.

Looking back on it I cannot see how I was able to do so many things
at once. I see that while all these excitements were going on I was
conducting for the Registrar of Restrictive Practices, first, a case about
the Doncaster and Retford Co-operative Societies agreement, and
second, a matter concerning the Wholesale Confectioners alliance of
Great Britain and Northern Ireland.

In the former case, a dull little matter suddenly became very exciting
when it transpired that the Secretary of the Parliamentary Committee
of the Co-operative Union had written an article in the *Co-operative
News* which suggested that it would be wrong for officials of co-operative societies to give evidence for the Registrar.

Poor Frank Soskice (now Lord Stow Hill) who had turned down the
Speakership of the House of Commons because he would not desert his
great friend Gaitskell, led for the Societies and was terribly embarrassed
by this disclosure, which, with typical candour, he himself made in
court.

The court took the matter very seriously.

'You have committed a gross contempt of court,' thundered Mr
Justice Diplock, (as he then was). 'This is a monstrous attempt to
influence the giving of evidence. We (he was sitting with four laymen,
one of whom was a trade unionist) have been considering whether the
proper course is not to inflict on you that punishment normally given

for contempt – imprisonment.'

The offender who had been called into the witness box by the Judge, wilted at the knees, grovelled, expressed his complete and unqualified apology to the court, and asked it to take a lenient course. Which, after suitable remarks about 'very severe punishment', it did.

That of course was a long time ago, and it is perhaps not without interest to see that I was leading a young man called Mr J. F. Donaldson. In his day, as the Judge presiding over the National Industrial Relations Court, the rule of law was no longer universally acknowledged. I am non-political and say no more.

The confectionery case was of absolutely no interest except to the wholesale confectionery trade who will not bulk large among my readers. I led the late Mr Justice Bagnall and Guy Aldous QC, the man who enquired before the war where Casko-Slavonika was(!) and who had become the leading silk at the patent bar, was for the Alliance.

He was and is a Master of Foxhounds, but his greatest claim to fame, to me at any rate, is that he is the possessor of the largest pair of feet I have ever seen. One day, a year or two ago, seeing him in the smoking room at the Inner Temple largely hidden (and large is the word) behind *The Times*, the feet only being visible, I ventured to say, 'And did those feet in ancient times?' whereupon he lowered his newspaper and replied, 'Yes, I had to sing that as a new boy at Harrow', and resumed his reading.

CHAPTER NINE

The Case of the Chief Constable

A week or two after *Meek* v *Fleming*, I started to argue the case for the defendants in *Ridge* v *Baldwin* and others, which eventually went to the House of Lords and which *The Times* newspaper has told us that the late Lord Reid regarded as his finest decision.

It was a complicated matter. Mr Ridge joined the police force in 1924 and the following year transferred to the county borough of Brighton, of which, after rising through all the ranks in the course of a long and distinguished career, he eventually became Chief Constable in July 1956. That was a very important and distinguished position which demanded the highest qualities of leadership and capacity for showing a good example to subordinates and setting a high standard of police conduct and behaviour.

Unhappily rumours got about that things were not well in this particular borough, and eventually there came about the embarrassing position that a team from another police force was discreetly keeping an eye on the local constabulary. When it was thought that sufficient evidence had been amassed, a prosecution was launched and in 1958 the Chief Constable found himself on trial at the Central Criminal Court, Old Bailey, before Mr Justice (later Lord) Donovan and a jury.

With him on one indictment were two police officers and two civilians on a charge of conspiracy to obstruct the course of public justice, while the second indictment charged him, alone, with corruption.

The trial of the first indictment went on for nineteen days at the end of which the two police officers were convicted but the Chief Constable was acquitted. The learned Judge in sentencing the two police officers said to them that facts admitted in the course of the trial 'establish that neither of you had that professional and moral leadership which both of you should have had and were entitled to expect from the Chief Constable.'

A week later the Chief Constable appeared at the Central Criminal

Court to answer the charge of corruption but no evidence was offered against him with the result that he left the court a free man. But before he left the learned Judge addressed some remarks to the Solicitor-General* who was prosecuting, referring to the particular police force and to the need for a new leader for it 'who will be a new influence and who will set a different example from that which has lately obtained'.

Well, a nod may be as good as a wink to a blind horse, but the Watch Committee (whose name is derived from the body of men who, before the institution of a police force, patrolled the street at night) were far from blind and had been following the case with the greatest concern. It is not surprising therefore that, that very night, the junior counsel on whom they normally relied was rung up at home and asked what they should do in the circumstances. It was a tricky one and it is impossible not to have sympathy with him, but he did not bring the Police Discipline Regulations of 1952 to the attention of the Watch Committee. I am not criticising him because in the event five judges held that he was right and four that he was wrong. Unfortunately for him, the four were all in the House of Lords.

So next day the Watch Committee met and in his absence, considered the length of the Chief Constable's service, the trial, the remarks of the Judge, and the statements the Chief Constable had made in evidence. They concluded that he had been negligent in the discharge of his duty and unfit for his post and dismissed him forthwith under the provisions of section 191(4) of the Municipal Corporations Act 1882. They returned his pension contribution.

Then there was some correspondence and some ten days later his solicitor addressed the committee, the majority of whom refused to change their minds. Then the Chief Constable appealed to the Home

---

* This was Sir Harry Hylton-Foster QC, whom we all used to call 'Hylton', who became Speaker of the House of Commons, and died young, tragically. We have what seems to me, who am not artistically talented, the most appalling painting of him in the Inner Temple. He was a tremendous admirer of Winston and had a very marginal seat at York.

I remember once saying that it seemed unwise to dismantle the base at Ismalia. 'Oh no!' he said, 'Winston says we can do it all from Cyprus'. Again, I said, 'Why don't we join in this Schumann plan for an European Defence Force?' 'Oh no!' was his reply, 'Winston says we can't do that; you see their standard of living is so much lower than ours. How would you like our soldiers to be paid the same as theirs?' When I became a judge he wrote to congratulate me, saying how suited I should be to dealing with undefended divorces (with which in fact I didn't deal), as he remembered how adept I had been at swatting flies at San Severo where we were together in 1944.

Secretary who found that there was sufficient material before the Watch Committee to justify the dismissal.

Many people would have given up at that point. But he had a terrier of a solicitor, a Mr Bosley, a very able man, who took the view that his client had been entitled to be dealt with in accordance with the Police Regulations, even though the Watch Committee might well have arrived at the same conclusion, if they had gone through the appropriate motions, as that which they in fact reached without such a journey. In other words, the cry went up that the Chief Constable had not received 'natural justice', two very emotive words for lawyers.

The Watch Committee, representing a very rich county borough, naturally went to the best man available, Gerald Gardiner. I may have had more newspapers than he had but he was the automatic first choice for anything like a *cause célèbre*. He never did any Restrictive Practices to my knowledge, although I think he led me for Fisons in the Monopolies Commission. But he had a colossal practice in those days and was, late in life, going into the Parliamentary and Town Planning work, which I regarded, probably out of envy because I never had any, as remunerative but boring.

Perhaps because of this new field of his, it transpired that he could not guarantee to do the case for the Watch Committee, and the brief came to me. I had quite a lot of briefs handed down from Gerald such as Keyes, and this one, and indeed later, in 1962, I had just finished doing a splendidly expensive case in which he had been originally instructed, when I was asked if I would like to be a Judge.

So I was never able to satisfy Bridget, who was determined that I should be the top man at the Bar. She used to keep all the snippets from the newspapers and paste them into scrap books. Very sweet of her and very boring work, but she did it right up to the date of my appointment and had she not done so it would have been impossible for me to have written this book.

I had enough of living in libraries when I did *Fraser on Libel* with Gerald Slade, as slave labour, in the thirties. I am writing this for fun and if I make a pound or two out of it, that will be pleasant, and more pleasant for the Inland Revenue who will have most of it. It is better to write with a scrap book by your side to jog your memory, looking at a beautiful view, with grandchildren screaming in the far background, than to labour after detail in a library.

Gerald Gardiner told me about the case as far as it had got. He was eight years older than I was, and of course it was not surprising that I couldn't catch him up and I never would have. He said that we had 'had it' as the Regulations obviously applied, and we hadn't followed them. It was as simple as that. He expressed his sympathy for the unfortunate junior. 'Too much for him; he would and perhaps will make an excellent stipendiary magistrate, but . . .' The junior was a dear who would have laughed, but he is no longer alive to do so. He never heard of this.

When the case came on I had spread all the papers over the dining table at June Farm and attempted to work out an argument to the effect that the Regulations didn't apply. To my surprise I succeeded in doing so. I didn't manage to convince myself, but I felt that if it could be demonstrated that perhaps a man didn't deserve to win, a judge might be ready to accept an argument that deprived him of victory.

Stanley Rees QC (later Mr Justice Rees and senior to me) made a stirring opening address at the end of which, the Judge having risen, he came across to me and invited me to make an offer of settlement. I would have been prepared to do so, but my clients were not, and I had to send him away empty-handed. My clients were more optimistic than I was, and it turned out that in the early stages they were right.

It must have been a very difficult decision whether or not to call the Chief Constable to give evidence and be cross-examined, as the issue on the uncontested facts seemed to me to be really one of law. I think that I would have called him, ascertained his name and address, and tendered him for cross-examination. He could not then have been cross-examined as to credit, for he would have said nothing to discredit. His solicitor could have brought out the fact that the Regulations had not been complied with, when he gave evidence.

However, I was given the chance of cross-examining him, and I soon realised that I was doing rather better than I had expected to do.

And by the time it came to the judgment which unfortunately I couldn't hear because I was in the House of Lords on another case (and there may be trouble if you don't turn up at the House of Lords), we were home.

'The plaintiff has been cross-examined in my court,' said Mr Justice Streatfeild, then 64 and very experienced, 'and my attention has been drawn to certain passages in the transcript of the trial. It would be blinding oneself to the facts of the case to come to any conclusion other than that, although acquitted, the plaintiff did not emerge from that trial without serious blots upon his escutcheon, and so thought the trial judge. Mr Justice Donovan's remarks could not be regarded as any kind of report or allegation to the Watch Committee. [NB. if they had been, that would have brought in the Police Regulations.] He was merely seeing that the curtain did not fall on the scenery following the plaintiff's acquittal, but that the limelight remained and the Watch Committee could view the scenery for themselves.' 'And', he continued, 'there could be no doubt on the admitted facts emerging from the evidence of the plaintiff himself that, although he was acquitted, his conduct indicated that he failed to display the necessary qualities of leadership and capacity to show an example, and there was ample evidence on which the Watch Committee could come to the conclusion that he was unfit to hold the appointment of Chief Constable.'

He went on to find that the Act of 1882 had not been repealed by the Police Act 1919 and the Police Discipline Regulations 1952 but that there was a state of peaceful co-existence between them.

He found that of course the plaintiff was entitled to natural justice but that in fact he had convicted himself out of this own mouth of unfitness to hold the office of Chief Constable and accordingly he had received natural justice.

And finally he held that even if the Chief Constable was right in saying that he should have been dismissed under the regulations, he had by appealing to the Secretary of State whose decision was said by the Act of 1882 to be final, waived the right to go to the High Court. We had won.

I was surprised and very pleased, but, more than that, there was jubilation among my clients. They invited me to a dinner to celebrate our great victory but I found an excuse not to go for I knew that this was only the quarter-final, although the judgment had seemed very convincing to me.

The semi-final was a success however. Three judges all well-known for their commonsense as well as their legal distinction heard the appeal : Lords Justice Pearce, Harman and Arthian Davies.

Neil Lawson QC (now Mr Justice Lawson) had taken over from Stanley Rees, and found an unsympathetic Bench.

They were determined to review this case from all admissible angles. And quite right too, I thought. In spite of Owlie Stable saying that a first trial is all about facts and in the Court of Appeal it is all about hypotheses, this court had the facts of the matter very firmly in mind. It was only when we got to the House of Lords that the facts seemed to be secondary, and we were dealing with abstract questions of law. (Owlie figures largely in Volume I and was a popular and human judge. He died, alas! in 1977.)

The judgment of the Court was delivered by Lord Justice (now Lord) Pearce. He is a man of parts, a very talented painter, and a marvellous after-dinner speaker who briefly filled the public eye a year or two ago when he went to Rhodesia on a fact-finding mission for the Government at great personal inconvenience and finanacial loss. He has twice been Master of the Skinners Company and some years ago retired from the Chairmanship of the Press Council.

He dealt with the matter succinctly. I apologise to those who are bored by this, but there may be some to whom the argument may be of interest.

He said that there were really four main questions to be determined. First, did the Watch Committee have power to dismiss the Chief Constable under the 1882 Act and, if so, did they have to follow the procedure under the Police Rules? Second, did the Watch Committee have to exercise the statutory power of dismissal in accordance with the principles of natural justice? Third, were the principles of natural justice in fact applied? And, fourth, did the appeal to the Home Secretary made by the Chief Constable under the Police Appeals Rules deprive him of his right to appeal to the High Court of Justice?

He said that Neil Lawson's contention that section 191 (4) of the Municipal Corporation Act 1882 had been repealed by implication was a bold assertion without authority to support it. He rejected it. The section was alive and the Watch Committee had power to dismiss under it.

As to how the statutory power was to be exercised by the Watch Committee, the Police Regulations did not apply and must be ignored. The act of the Watch Committee was administrative, and they could 'hire and fire' (actually he said 'appoint and dismiss') at their discretion. They were not obliged to make an inquiry of a judicial or quasi-judicial nature and there was no infringement of natural justice.

In making his appeal to the Home Secretary, the Chief Constable had accepted that the Home Secretary's decision would be final and binding, and accordingly he could not be heard to come before the High Court.

The other two Lords Justice agreed and leave to appeal to the House of Lords was refused. The ratepayers no doubt felt that the costs of the defence were justified. All the same, I felt very worried when I heard that Neil Lawson, who is a first-class lawyer, was to be instructed by the indefatigable Mr Bosley to apply to the Appeals Committee of the House of Lords for leave to petition for the decision of the Court of Appeal to be reversed.

Whether the Chief Constable was legally aided or whether he had some trade union behind him I didn't know, but it looked as though money was no object. The Watch Committee did not take me in at this hearing. Leave was granted.

'Hard cases make bad law', was what I feared was going to be argued. That is to say, if you stretch the law in order to do what you conceive to be justice in a particular case, you may be setting up a precedent which will result in injustice in some future case, or at least you may be making it very difficult for lawyers to advise their clients as to what the law will be declared to be in any particular case.

When a case is heard in the rarefied atmosphere of their Lordships' House the facts are liable to be treated mainly from the angle of the fascinating points of law which they raise, and rightly so. It may be that expediency ruled their Lordships' minds in what Lord Reid called 'the very peculiar decision of their Lordships' House in *Liversidge* v *Anderson'*, a wartime case concerning internment under S.18(b), or again in *R.* v *Joyce,* Lord Haw-Haw of infamous memory : but these cases are rare indeed.

I feel that I might have had more chance if Lord Denning had been sitting, and indeed Lord Evershed was with me from the start, but there were four other stony faces turned towards me when I rose to answer my opponent's argument. Presiding was Lord Reid, the most formidable figure of them all, who occupied the chair until the age of eighty-four. Neil Lawson (as I later learnt) was becalmed in the Court of Appeal and because of this had to return the brief at the last moment, and I was faced by Desmond Ackner QC (now Mr Justice Ackner), who had only recently taken silk.

He ran rings round me from the start, citing a number of cases which had not been relied on before, working all through the night. I remember one morning coming into the robing room in the Lords, having travelled gently up from the country and enjoyed a quiet constitutional up Victoria Street from the station, pleased with myself for having finished *The Times,* which seemed to have a lot in it that day, to find this little dynamo reading some law report, which he had dug up in the Middle Temple Library in the middle of the night, and shaving with his electric razor as he walked up and down the room.

(That was a great day for me : I went to Remington and I have shaved in bed ever since.)

He seemed to produce new cases like a conjuror, and when Lord Reid said quietly that some of those cases (which he produced during his Reply) seemed to have more bearing on the point than some others to which their Lordships had had to listen, I began to lose hope. Lord Devlin, as was his wont, asked one or two deceptively simple questions which were traps to be avoided with care. Lord Evershed who had made up his mind in my favour on the first day, 'that there was no real substantial miscarriage of justice', was not listening, and Lord Morris of Borth-y-Gest and Lord Hodson were listening and saying nothing. But they seemed to be listening to my opponent with approval.

In the end we lost by 4 to 1 : the appeal was allowed with costs and the case was remitted to the Queen's Bench Division. It was then settled, I know not upon what terms, and Desmond and Mr Bosley had won a very fine victory. What it must have cost the ratepayers, I shudder to think, and the Chief Constable, who had to wait some five years for his money, deserves some sympathy.

By the time that their Lordships delivered judgment I had already become a judge so that I did not have to attend to hear the speeches. It was interesting however to read that the dismissal of the appellant was null and void, but that it was right to put on record that he did not seek to be reinstated as Chief Constable. One would have thought that if his dismissal was null and void he still was Chief Constable. But no doubt Lord Reid insisted on that term.

CHAPTER TEN

Mr Mann and Dr Barbara Moore

Immediately after the first hearing of the Chief Constable's case I appeared for the plaintiff in a case, which was then of topical interest, where my client, Mr Mann, sued Shell Petroleum, for whom Gerald Gardiner appeared, for remuneration which was said to have been earned as a result of a visit to Cuba to protect the interests of the defendants.

What happened was that after the Castro revolt had toppled the Batista government in 1958 all things British became unpopular and a boycott was imposed on British goods. Shell in particular were unpopular, because it was said that Mr Inglesia, the chairman of Shell in Cuba, had assisted in the purchase from an English company of twelve aeroplanes for the Batista government when that government had no aircraft. This could not have happened without a licence from the British Government. Mr Inglesia had to resign, there was a boycott imposed, and a representative of Shell was refused an interview with Dr Castro.

Shell then asked my man, who was named Mann, to help. He was a stateless Rumanian who knew everybody. Not unlike the egregious Mr Stanley of Lynskey Tribunal fame, except that Mr Mann was honest and Mr Stanley was not. Indeed, as Gardiner made a direct attack on his honour and credibility, the Judge had to deal with that point. He said that it was necessary to state that Mr Mann was basically an honest man, very well thought of in the commercial world and a reasonably credible witness who could without difficulty have invented a more favourable interview with Doctor Castro than the one he described, had he wished to lie.

Mr Mann arrived in Cuba on 3rd February 1959 and had a very satisfactory interview with Dr Castro, to whom he put a proposition under which he would get £100 million from the United Kingdom. Castro said, 'Do not worry. Everything will be all right.' He asked

Mr Mann to go next day to the Shell refinery where he was to make a speech, and he put his car at the plaintiff's disposal. Castro, as is his habit, spoke for three hours and the boycott was lifted. He sent for the plaintiff and embraced him.

'Contented?' he asked.

'Very contented', replied the plaintiff.

His evidence was supported by Sir Stanley Rawson, a distinguished industrialist who had been a Fellow of All Souls, Commander Michael Parker, and a Senor Pazos.

It all seemed to be going swimmingly. But the defence which, in the absence of Castro as a witness, was difficult to refute, was that when Dr Castro raised the boycott it was on the terms agreed upon by the management of the Cuban Company and the workers at a meeting held before the unfortunate plaintiff had even arrived in Havana. And the Judge accepted that defence, whilst sympathising with my man, who had done all he could without knowing of the the previous bargain between the management and the workers. He said that it might have been that Castro had given the plaintiff the impression that it was he who had effected the lifting of the embargo. He also said that he had been within an ace of succeeding on behalf of the British Consortium, and that through no fault of his, a shift in the political situation had caused those negotiations to come to nothing.

But that didn't help much. And so the plaintiff lost, and the £5,000 in court, paid in by Shell, was paid out to them.

It seemed very bad luck. The public embracing by Castro must have given the impression that Mann had played his part, and it did seem very strange to me that Shell should not have informed their emissary on his arrival in Cuba that they had already settled the dispute, and that his services accordingly were no longer required.

The solicitor for Mr Mann, who wanted to appeal although I advised him not to, seemed satisfied with my efforts for he then wished to instruct me in a fashionable divorce case in which Gardiner was to be against me.

One Sunday morning the solicitor rang me up in bed to enquire why my clerk had refused the brief and told me in flattering terms how his client's father was so anxious that I should take the case against Gardiner, as he knew that I was the man for the job, and so forth. After a while I asked him when the case was to come on. He told me the date that had been fixed. I said that now I understood:

I should be in the Court of Appeal on that date and what was more, Gardiner would be against me. The relief was obvious from the tone of voice at the other end of the telephone, and the conversation terminated in the most friendly manner. All that was required was that either I should take on Gerald, or that he should not be there. If he was not to be there, it was perfectly satisfactory to leave the case to the 2nd XI !

In August 1961 I had another case in which Sir Stanley Rawson, whom I have just mentioned, was also concerned, in which I was instructed by Messrs Slaughter & May. This was rather grand, for it was a company matter, and up till then Messrs. Slaughter & May had only patronised me in defamation cases. I did not however allow this to go to my head, as I realised that in all probability counsel of their first choice were away on holiday as it was the Long Vacation. The case was an application by a gentleman who had been the managing director and moving spirit in a company, (and had been removed from that position, becoming a non-executive director), to commit to Brixton Prison (it is Pentonville nowadays) five very distinguished fellow directors for alleged contempt of court. The Vacation Judge was a new judge, Mr Justice Widgery, whom we last met in my first book in the Watford County Court, and who is now The Lord Chief Justice of England. He disposed of the case with expedition in three days and dismissed our opponent's motion with costs.

In that year I was in a couple of political libel actions. One was for Mr Solly Sachs, then the prospective Labour candidate for Hallam, Sheffield and best known for his life-long opposition to apartheid in South Africa. He took £3,000 and indemnity costs from the *Jewish Chronicle*. Mr Peter Bristow, who had been with me in the Anders case, did the apologising.

The other was for Mr Humphrey Berkeley MP, then a Conservative, (now a Socialist) against Beaverbrook Newspapers, for whom Gerald Gardiner had a retainer. Gerald apologised for the *Sunday Express* and agreed to pay £1,500 and indemnity costs.

I began two great cases in 1961, *Rookes* v *Barnard,* and *Lewis* v *Associated Newspapers* and *Lewis* v *Daily Telegraph Ltd*. The latter two cases I treat as one for reasons which will appear hereafter.

But before I come to these two marathon matters in both of which the House of Lords delivered judgment after I was on the Bench and in one of which I did not even argue the case in the House of Lords, I must say a word or two about Dr Barbara Moore.

Doctor Barbara Nicolaevna Moore was a very remarkable woman. She was only fifty-five when her action against the *Daily Mail* was heard in July 1961. It was then that she told me in cross-examination that there was no reason why she should not have a child at the age of one hundred, and said that she did not expect to get older than she was then, for the next hundred years. Alas : she has now died at a mere seventy-one. She seemed to be entirely sincere if a little eccentric. But then Galileo was considered very eccentric indeed in his time.

Born in Russia in 1906, she obtained a degree in medicine but did not practise, apart from one year in a Russian hospital. She left Russia when she was twenty-seven and was at that time a conventional vegetarian. In India, however, she decided on a fruit, vegetable and nut diet. The next year, 1934, saw her arrival in England where in 1946 after the war she started her quest for eternal youth. She wished to establish how far it was possible to live a healthy life without eating at all, or at any rate eating only a minimum. She took the view that foods outside her diet were impure, and that elderly people, spared from the effort of digesting such food, would be more active and live much longer than the normal life span. So she went to the Alps between 1946 and 1954 where she ate very little, finally subsisting on liquids from raw vegetables and fruit before she began mountain-climbing. During her mountain-climbing period she fasted for ninety days. Mountain-climbing in Switzerland being a strenuous occupation, it was perhaps not surprising that by 1953 she became listless and in 1954 felt that she had not long to live. By 1958, however, she began to recover and was well again in October of that year.

She then decided that she could prove that her diet theories were correct and that a properly trained body would withstand tremendous strain more effectively by publicity in England than by returning to Switzerland.

So she walked from Birmingham to London and did it in twenty-seven hours. That was six and a half hours less than some servicemen had taken. It was suggested that she must have taken a lift. That displeased her, and she did the walk again in even shorter time. She then walked from Edinburgh to London in seven days.

By this time, her activities were well publicised and the public was very interested, whether because she was 'a symbol of raw eating', as she herself put it, or whether because she was a very remarkable long-distance walker and a female at that, one cannot tell.

But when it was announced that she intended to walk from John O'Groats to Land's End, she became temporarily a national figure. She walked through blizzards and was soaked by rain and had very little sleep, breakfasting and dining on chopped raw cabbage, and having honey as a principal item of diet. Between John O'Groats and Fort William she was escorted by a van voluntarily provided by the North of Scotland Milk Marketing Board. This must have been the worst part of the journey, and the van was presumably provided in case of emergencies.

Then a van provided by the Calor Gas Company appeared, unsolicited. They proceeded together as far as Wellington, Shropshire, where she said in evidence that the driver dumped her spare clothing on the pavement and drove back to Scotland. When she had got to Bristol a van from the Dunlop Rubber Company began to escort her. She had been to the Dunlop premises in Liverpool before the walk and had accepted, on the terms that there were no strings attached, four pairs of yachting shoes, two pairs of baseball shoes, and two pairs of tennis shoes for which the company declined to allow her to pay.

Her case was that the Dunlop shoes were not very satisfactory, but that the Dunlop driver was very helpful. He had told her that Dunlops were going to have an advertisement about the walk in the *Daily Mail*. This worried her and she asked to see a proof, but she never did. Later on a man gave her two oranges which she accepted saying, 'I hope there are no strings attached'. She then found two crates of oranges in the van and a cheque for £10. She didn't cash the cheque but she ate some of the oranges.

The *Daily Mail* published a feature headed 'Salute to Dr Moore'. In the feature, advertising space had been taken by Dunlops, among others.

It looked inocent enough, but Dr Moore issued a writ claiming that the feature meant that she had walked from John O'Groats to Land's End for financial gain and that she had been dishonest and insincere when she had stated that her purpose was to prove as a scientific fact that a woman of her age could walk such a distance on an exclusive diet of raw foods.

The newspaper knew that she had written an autobiography, and that she had received a fee of £3,000 for its publication in serial form in the *People* after she had re-written it. They had a photograph of her posing with Dunlop representatives before a Dunlop van at Land's End, and another lying in bed with a pair of Dunlop shoes on the counterpane. They knew that they had paid her 26 guineas for an article on longevity and that their sister newspaper the *Daily Sketch* had paid £50 when they had lost a bet with her of that amount that she would not do the Birmingham-London walk a second time. And they knew that the feature complained of contained only one advertisement which suggested that she had used the advertiser's goods, and that was by Dunlop.

And finally, they had a statement from an executive of Dunlops to the effect that early in the walk in Lancashire the Doctor had told him that she had no objection to Dunlops taking space in the feature in question.

It seemed to the newspaper that it was difficult to say that it was an immoral thing to be sponsored by the *Daily Mail*, whereas it was proper to accept a large sum of money from the *People*, which clearly would not have been paid unless she had successfully completed this remarkable feat of endurance.

And they put in a defence saying that the words were not defamatory; alternatively that she had impliedly consented to the publication of two of the advertisements in the feature.

I scored a few techincal points for the newspaper which are of no general interest. Mr Justice McNair*, a distinguished commercial lawyer, was interested in them and summed up to the jury in a manner of which I could make no complaint, and the Doctor had not done herself justice in the witness box. We thought that we might have won, but we hadn't. The jury disbelieved the man from Dunlops and accepted the plaintiff's case, put forward with much charm and grace by the present Mr Justice Dunn, who was then a junior. They awarded £1,000 and by reason of my little technical triumphs (or because he thought that we ought to have won) the Judge only awarded her half her costs. I don't say the jury were wrong, and I cannot, as we did not appeal. But I did feel a little disappointed.

Years afterwards, when she had demonstrated by her extraordinary conduct in subsequent litigation in which I was not concerned, but in which poor Buster Milmo bore the brunt, that she was 'round the bend', Robin Dunn actually told me that she went off her head because I had halved her costs. I was astonished.

*Now Sir William McNair, aged eighty-six.

CHAPTER ELEVEN

A Blow for Freedom

In 1956, Douglas Edwin Rookes was a bachelor of thirty-eight, employed by BOAC in the drawing office at London Airport at £884 p.a. rising to £1,092 p.a., with generous travel facilities and very cheap fares of which he took frequent advantage. He lost his job on 16th March 1956 and it was not until 1963 that the proceedings consequent thereupon were terminated. The decision of the House of Lords caused the Socialist Party to enact fresh legislation, and even today the issue is still to some extent in the melting pot following further legislation by the great Parliamentary parties.

It was in his speech in this case that Lord Devlin set out the limited number of occasions when it is proper to award exemplary damages. Australia refused to follow this, and the Privy Council has declared that *Rookes* v *Barnard* forms no part of the law of Australia. The Court of Appeal has held that the doctrine in *Rookes* v *Barnard* as to exemplary damages was expressed wrongly and *per incuriam* (which is a polite Latin way of saying that the House was asleep at the time) and that the law of England is the same as that of Australia; and the House of Lords has held that the remarks of the Court of Appeal were quite wrong, and possibly impertinent as well.

For my part, I do not think the law is satisfactory and that whilst we should still retain the concept of aggravated compensatory damages, Parliament ought to legislate for the abolition of punitive, exemplary, and deterrent damages – the three adjectives being to my mind synonymous. If you must fine a defendant for bad behaviour, surely the State rather than the plaintiff should benefit.

Whatever else happens to him and he is only sixty if he, as I hope, is still alive, Mr Rookes will surely go down to legal history.

He was the victim of a conspiracy by members of the Association of Engineering and Shipbuilding Draughtsmen, and it is an indication of the complexity of the law on this subject that whereas six judges agreed with me, three were persuaded to take a different view although there was no dispute as to the facts.

I will try to condense those facts which are not very simple.

On 1st April 1949 there came into force at Heathrow Airport an agreement between the employers' and employees' side of the Panel of the National Joint Council for civil air transport, by which *no strike action should take place,* and disputes should be dealt with by negotiation.

At the same time there was an understanding between the Union and BOAC referred to as the '100 per cent membership agreement'. Its terms were that once a declaration of 100% membership had been made by a union and accepted by the corporation, there was a 'closed shop', and BOAC would not thereafter recruit any non-Union staff for that section or union *and* that a member of the union was not, after the declaration, under an obligation to remain in it, could resign, and would not thereby lose his employment.

The design office in which Rookes was employed, was the subject of a 100% declaration as far back as 1951. He was a member of the union and at one time a shop steward. He was no Uncle Tom but a militant (and the law should be the same for both). He took the view that the union was taking insufficient action over drawing-office accommodation, and threatened to and did resign in November 1955.

Mr Silverthorne, a London divisional organiser of the union, who was the second defendant, and who died before the case went to the Court of Appeal, called Rookes a 'blackleg' and an 'anarchist' and said, 'If you don't return we'll bring the whole of BOAC to a standstill'. He wrote a letter on 9th December 1955 saying that Rookes should be discharged by BOAC if he did not rejoin the union. In cross-examination by me he said, somewhat lamely, that he did not mean that, but only that he should be removed from the office. He made his views clear when the Judge asked him if a man could resign from the union if he was genuinely fed up. 'He ought not to,' he replied.

Mr Barnard, the first defendant, was the chairman of the Feltham, Middlesex branch of the union, and had spoken in support of strike action although, as he said, he knew that strike action would be in breach of contract with the employers.

Mr Fistal was the shop steward in the drawing-office when Rookes resigned. He was the third defendant and thought it very important that the 100% office membership should be maintained. He agreed that the threatened strike would have been in breach of the agreement with BOAC and that Rookes would not have lost his job if he and his friends had not threatened the strike.

None of these three distinguished themselves in the witness box.

Rookes had wanted to talk to the other members of the drawing-office to express his point of view, but the defendants would not allow it for 'he had contracted out of union membership and thus denied himself the facility of union meeting!'

Then the support of other unions was enlisted; by 4th January 1956 threats of strike action were in the air, and later the BOAC personnel manager was handed a union resolution which said that if Rookes were not removed, union members would be withdrawn. Such withdrawal would have been a gross breach of their written agreement with their employers, but they didn't care; it was just a piece of paper.

This was an early example of the rule of the jungle defeating the rule of law, and unhappily not a solitary example. The union had BOAC 'over a barrel' like Mr Jackson of the Gordon Hotels cases. They had a meeting and BOAC capitulated. Rookes was sent home on paid leave on 13th January, and dismissed by BOAC on 16th March.

Before Rookes was actually dismissed, it was thought a good idea to make allegations of misconduct against him, so that he could be removed without it being apparent that it was the union which had got him the sack. BOAC agreed to hold an inquiry.

BOAC took the view which Lord Reid had expressed in the Chief Constable's case that on an inquiry into misconduct by a servant it was quite a good wrinkle to let both sides say their little piece, and they notified Rookes of the hearing. This was the most important matter in his life and he got there early. Later Mr Fistal and three other members of the union, none of whom worked in Rookes' particular section, put in an appearance, saw that Rookes was there, and marched off again. As you may imagine, I had some fun with that in cross-examination, and I have no doubt that the jury took a very low view of such behaviour. (I wasn't able, try though I did, to refer to any of this in the Court of Appeal, although I assume that their Lordships read the transcripts.)

The witness from BOAC said, categorically, that Rookes would not have been removed from the office, had there been no threat to withdraw labour.

Those were the agreed facts. The plaintiff had dared to resign from his union and had lost his livelihood in consequence, for after his dismissal the only appointment he had been offered had been in English Electric. He had refused that, as it meant work on military aircraft, because he held strong pacifist views. As a result he lost his unemployment benefit and he was living on such savings as he had.

Most men would have thrown up the sponge, and taken the job with English Electric. Some would have gone to a solicitor to ask what chance they had of obtaining damages. The odds are that they would have been told, 'My dear sir, there are two classes of people in this country – the trades unions and their members, and the unfortunate rest of us. They are above the law, we are subject to it. I'm afraid that they can do as they like and you must toe the line.'

Somehow or other, Mr Rookes went to a family firm of solicitors who are Socialist politicians, and they took the case and managed to get him legal aid. Lord Silkin was held in high esteem on both sides of the House, and was even considered to have shifted slightly to the right after he reached the Lords. He was largely responsible for the New Towns set up under Mr Attlee's government which as far as I know – and I don't know very much – have been a success. Of two of his sons, one was allocated to me as junior and the other was my instructing solicitor, although I never met him. They are both now in the Government, my junior as Attorney-General, the other as Minister of Agriculture.

I have no idea what the political opinions of my junior and his brother may have been in 1961. They were of no interest to a non-political person like me. But it does show how important it is, as I have written before, to keep one's profession and one's politics separate.

Denis Pritt QC of the London Electricity Board case (see *No Mitigating Circumstances*), could never do that. Serjeant Sullivan QC (R.C.) and Lord Caldecote (Low Church) would never have changed sides in custody cases, but I think it is rather good that here was Sam Silkin supporting me for an individual David slinging away against a Goliath union, when his political convictions, and those of his brother, may well have been out of sympathy with his client.

(I subscribed to *Private Eye*. In an issue a year or two ago, on the page after the cover, a passage read,

George Cunningham, Labour M.P. for Islington South, has been investigating the activities of ———, estate agents.

During his investigation, Mr Cunningham received a threatening letter from ——— 's, solicitors. None other than the old-established socialist firm of Lewis Silkin and Partners. Senior partner, Rt Hon John Silkin PC, MP, the Minister for Planning.

If that is to be read as an attack on the solicitor, because he also happens to be a Minister, it seems to me to be a little unfair.)

I was out of sympathy with my client too, although I fought for him with all that I had in me. In my Blimpish way, I don't care for bearded pacifists, and I told him I didn't think an English jury would, either, and I forecast much lower damages than he was later awarded. But the enemy were really so unattractive in the witness box that we easily beat the £1,500 paid into court.

If I may be forgiven a dissertative parenthesis, I appeared in 1962 on one occasion for the ETU then under right wing management by Mr Cannon and Mr Chapple, the former now dead but the latter happily still in the saddle. This was after the defeat of the Communist faction of Mr Foulkes and Mr Hazell who had been found guilty by Mr Justice Winn of fraudulent manipulation of the ballot for General Secretary.

In the same year I appeared for the *Daily Worker* against Sir Oswald Mosley, who appeared in person to apply for an interlocutory injunction against the newspaper. He failed.

I had no hesitation about taking both those briefs and had I been a political animal I should have felt the same. It would be a bad day when a member of the Bar was accused of insincerity for appearing professionally to espouse a cause with which he was not in sympathy. On the other hand, I think you are entitled to say, 'Of course, I will appear for you, the *Daily Worker,* but I should say that I have no sympathy with your political views and shall understand if you go else-where.'

In the same way Gerald Gardiner made plain his personal dis-approval of the late Lord Beaverbrook in *Waugh* v *Spain,* but acted with absolute propriety in appearing for Beaverbrook Newspapers until he became Lord Chancellor. The man and the advocate must at all costs be kept distinct.

Before I come back to *Rookes* v *Barnard* may I say that when I cross-examined Sir Oswald Mosley it was only the third time that I had seen him; once as best man at a wedding when my sister was a bridesmaid, where he naturally stole the show in his Fascist uniform which I didn't like; once at the Albert Hall in similar costume where he made an extremely impressive speech, but his acolytes were dreadful men, and I thought it quite right when he was locked up under Regulation 18 (b) as a danger to the country; and this last time.

I was amazed. If ever there was a man you would have been honoured and pleased to ask to dinner that was he. The Master of the Rolls said that he had put his case with great moderation, ability and skill. I thought that an understatement.

In Rookes's case I felt that the jury were against the defendants and also that, in view of the well-known habit of juries of awarding too much out of a sense of disgust with the defendants, rather than in order to compensate the plaintiff reasonably for his sufferings, I ought to say something about the amount of damages. I knew that Mr Justice Sachs would be bound to do so even if I did not, so that there would be no harm in it.

Before the case started the Judge had said that, if any of the jury lived in or around Heathrow Airport, he would be prepared to give careful consideration to any applications to be excused from serving on this case. No one did apply, but it seemed to me that the Judge (of blackboard fame in the pottery case described in Volume I) had done a lot of homework and decided that emotions might be aroused.

So I urged them to award a reasonable sum by telling them all about the Greeks and the classical doctrine of Meden Agan (Nothing to excess). And then the Judge said it all over again in his summing up in English, so that it didn't hurt.

While the jury were out John Thompson QC, who was against me, and who became a Judge before we got to the Court of Appeal, came to me and said, 'Tell me, what was the point of all that Greek? What had it got to do with it?'

I said, 'Not much, but they like a change, and I did say I was proud to be the last advocate to talk Greek to a jury.'

He was not amused, and I don't suppose that anyone else would have been, but I was thinking of the late Mr Justice Charles who, when someone threw an obscure Latin tag at him, retorted, 'Don't you talk Greek to me.'

The jury returned and gave Mr Rookes £7,500. Then we had a fortnight's suspense while the Judge considered whether, even so, the

union (and its officials also) were protected by sections 1 and 3 of the
Trade Disputes Act 1906.

He returned in due course and in a judgment which I, humbly,
thought admirable, rejected the submission of the union.

There was a hullabaloo. The papers naturally made the most of it,
and Mr George Woodcock, the TUC Secretary, very sensibly said,
'I cannot comment until I know more about it. A lot of questions are
raised. We will have to see the whole of the judgment and get counsel's
opinion before saying this has general application.'

Nevertheless, one national newspaper said :

Britain's 8 million trade unionists will have to stop assuming that
they can call lightning strikes, or threaten a man if he refuses to
join their union, without facing heavy damages.

This was an exciting misconception of the position which Messrs.
Silkin put correctly, 'The decision does not mean that the closed shop
itself is illegal. The only things in dispute were the particular methods
by which a closed shop was called into force.'

'This means that unions', added the *Daily Mail,* who got it right,
'who have "no-strike" or other agreements with employers, will find
themselves handicapped in backing up closed shop demands.'

'If they break (and the newspaper should have added : 'or threaten
to break') those agreements in order to enforce their demands, then
they are acting illegally and are open to legal action.'

When the Judge had finished his judgment, I hoped that the
unfortunate Rookes would receive the £7,500 and costs awarded.
Not a bit of it. The union was going to the Court of Appeal; there
was £1,500 in court and that would do for the time being.

The Judge said that another £1,000 should be brought into court
and we were then told that this would involve approaches to the
defendants' fellow workmen and that a collection might have to be
made. It all seemed unreal. The plaintiff was lucky enough to be
legally aided which meant that he got the best legal representation
without paying anything at all, whereas the defendants were supported
by a union which was prepared to give them the best legal representation without their paying anything at all. But when the matter had
been ventilated for a very long time at the greatest expense and the
defendants had lost, the union had apparently no power to advance

more than £500 per defendant, and the wretched plaintiff could fish for the rest, and for the costs.

However, the Judge was not to be moved, and as the case did go to the Court of Appeal, I can only assume the union managed to scratch up the odd £1,000 somewhere.

Lest I be thought conceited, I should point out that I should have said that Mr Rookes *may* have had the best legal representation available. In fact the solicitors first went to Sir Hartley Shawcross, who produced the most erudite opinion on the law, of many pages, upon which eventually I based my opening address to the jury, as I take the view that you must immediately let them into the secret of what you say the law is, otherwise they are blundering about and bored stiff.

So I told them in opening how Mr Justice Harman had said in *Huntley* v *Thornton* 1957 1 WLR 321 that, if all the defendants had done was to inform the employers that the continued employment of the plaintiff would have untoward results, they did no more than they were entitled to do, but that if their actions amounted to threats of illegal strike action to withdraw labour in breach of contract, those acts were tortious and illegal.

I had got that case from Shawcross's opinion. He had become ennobled and had left the Bar for a great commercial career, and the solicitors then went to Sir Milner Holland who had led me for Jackson at the Old Bailey. He wasn't a common law man any more than he was a criminal lawyer but he would have known the Trade Disputes Act inside out, and was an admirable choice. Unhappily for Rookes, perhaps, but happily for me, he was very busy, he and Sir Andrew Clark being at that time the two undisputed leaders of the Chancery Bar. He, Milner, never became a judge because he didn't want it. He used to say that he'd never be able to enjoy himself at a cocktail party if he became a stuffy old judge. I am sure that he could have been a judge if he had so desired. He once told me that what he really wanted was to be a Privy Councillor. But, sadly, that never happened.

As a result of his being so busy, the case eventually devolved on me. The papers showed no sign of any industry on his part. Probably, he, too, was content to fashion his case around Lord Shawcross's opinion.

I knew that the union had taken in Gerald Gardiner to lead in the Court of Appeal as Colin Duncan in my chambers, who was the union's junior throughout, told me so.

When we arrived at the Court of Appeal, Gardiner opened the case at a tremendous rate of knots, so that he had finished quoting one case and passed on to the next before I had found my place in the first one. How the Court of Appeal kept up with him, I don't know. I certainly couldn't.

It was all very dramatic to start with, when he told their Lordships that Mr Justice Sachs had driven a coach and four through the Trade Disputes Act 1906 (a phrase which had been used when *Hyams* v *Stuart King*, which we killed in *Hill* v *Hill* [in the first volume] performed the same equestrian feat with regard to the Gaming and Wagering Act). He seemed to suggest that the trade unions could do anything they liked, however abominably they behaved, because of the protection of Sections 1 and 3 of the 1906 Act.

And that was just what he did mean. He didn't challenge any of the findings of the jury that each of the three defendants had :

(1)   been a party to a conspiracy to threaten strike action by members of the AESD against BOAC to secure the withdrawal of the plaintiff from the design office

(2)   made a threat to take strike action against BOAC to secure that withdrawal, and

(3)   caused the dismissal of the plaintiff by those threats of strike action.

But he said that the union and its members were free from legal action, even though they had threatened to break a binding contract in order to attain their desires.

I couldn't imagine that the Court of Appeal would buy that one; but buy it they did. In vain, I pointed out that all these men had to do, instead of threatening to break their contract illegally, was to say, 'You know, if this man remains in the office, I am afraid that we shall have to give you a week's notice.'

In vain, I attempted to draw their Lordships' attention to the merits of the case. But the merits were neither here nor there, for had not Mr Gardiner pointed out in opening that this was a pure point of law, and that he could not understand why the three defendants were called to be put through the hoop by Mr Neville Faulks. In vain, did I flourish an article in a learned journal by Professor Hamson of Cambridge University (whose suitcase Bridget had been lumbered with in Finkelbaum times) to the effect that Sachs J. had got it right, for Gerald Gardiner had an article by a left-wing don at Clare called Wedderburn who said the opposite, and who now is at the London

School of Economics and has recently become Lord Wedderburn of Charlton, and often writes to *The Times*. We gave the court both articles to take away with them when they reserved judgment. That they did for a very long time. Terence Donovan came up to me one day and said that he took a couple of the relevant law reports to bed with him every night but still had not stumbled on the truth. I felt like asking if Lady D. objected, but held my tongue.

Lord Justice Sellers gave the leading judgment with which his colleagues agreed. He told the world that the clear answer to the plaintiff's claim was that there was no actionable wrong, for the plaintiff had not established a conspiracy to injure him. The predominant purpose of the conspiracy, believe it or not, being the legitimate promotion of the interests of the persons combining.

Sam Silkin had followed me and done very well, and I was glad that he was there to take the judgment, and not I, for he is more phlegmatic than I am, and I might have made some tactless observation about what seemed to me to be a monstrous miscarriage of justice.

We went to the Lords, thanks to the Legal Aid Scheme. Sam Silkin did it by himself and won, after many vicissitudes. I was following it as a distant spectator having become a judge and have no idea of how the tide flowed during the argument. All I know is that one of their Lordships, without committing himself, prepared me for disaster, and Colin Duncan and Gerald Gardiner looked uncommonly pleased with themselves. Then the great Lord Reid reconvened the tribunal, heard further argument and at last they came out with what I thought to be the sane solution. The appeal was allowed, and judgment was entered for Rookes. But the coda was Lord Devlin's speech about damages to which I have already referred : accordingly, when Rookes went to see Neil Lawson he must have had excellent advice and I believe, although I do not know, that he finally settled for much less than £7,500. Poor fellow.

I am given to clichés, and I would like to call that case 'A Blow for Freedom'. It is all in the Law Reports, and when I tell you that the vital matter was the word 'only' in section 3 of the 1906 Act, you may be happy that I have not explained the legal difficulties in adequate detail.

I hope however that I have shown where the merits lay.

CHAPTER TWELVE

Copycat Damages

In the nineteen fifties, there were two Socialist MPs called Lewis who had distinguished themselves, or at least had caught the public eye, and the ordinary newspaper reader was liable to get mixed up as to which was which.

One of them had decided to lie down in Savoy Hill, or somewhere adjacent, in order to demonstrate to his constituents his support of some union or other which was in dispute with the Savoy Hotel. I think that the idea was to obstruct the delivery of supplies. He was not run over, and the demonstration (I suppose it would be called a 'one man demo' today) attracted much popular attention. The other gentleman with whose legal affairs I became involved, had attracted the finger of fame by having an altercation with a police constable who had the audacity to stop him in the Mall while he was on his way to conduct the country's business as an elected member of Her Majesty's House of Commons.

This was Mr John Lewis who was the chairman and managing director of a company called Rubber Improvements Ltd. which carried on a large business in the plastics and rubber industries. On 17th July 1961 he was not fifty years of age but had been a Member of Parliament for six years and Parliamentary Secretary to the Postmaster General in the Labour administration. He was a liveryman of two City companies, a racehorse owner, and a former member of the British Boxing Board of Control. His company had a capital of one million pounds and more than three thousand shareholders.

In *The Daily Telegraph* on the front page on 23rd December 1958, the season of goodwill, appeared :

INQUIRY ON FIRM BY CITY POLICE

Officers of the City of London Fraud Squad are inquiring into the affairs of Rubber Improvements Ltd. and its subsidiary companies. The investigation was requested after criticisms of the chairman's statement and the accounts by a shareholder at the recent Company Meeting.

The chairman of the company which has an authorised capital of £1m, is Mr John Lewis, former Socialist M.P. for Bolton.*

Mr Lewis said that the words meant that he had been guilty or was suspected by the police of having been guilty of fraud or dishonesty in connection with the affairs of his company, or that he had caused or permitted the affairs of the company and its subsidiaries to be conducted fraudulently or dishonestly.

The company said that the article meant that their affairs and those of their subsidiaries were conducted fraudulently or dishonestly or in such a way that the police suspected that their affairs were so conducted, because it was generally known that the City Fraud Squad investigated serious cases of company fraud.

We – I appeared for the newspaper with Mr Hugh Davidson – did not agree. We thought that my old friend, Colin Duncan, who was the junior against me in *Rookes* v *Barnard,* had thoroughly over-egged the pudding with all these alleged meanings. It was plainly stated that a shareholder had made criticisms, and there was no doubt about that because Mr Milmo said so in his opening speech, and that, as a result, there was an inquiry by the Fraud Squad into the affairs of the company. I called a Detective-Sergeant of the City of London Fraud Squad who said that on 25th November 1958 he was instructed to search the national and local records in respect of Mr John Lewis and Rubber Improvements Ltd. and its associated group of companies. He said he would not have been asked to do so had there not been an inquiry afoot.

Mr Lewis went into the witness box and told the jury that he was a liveryman of two city companies and a racehorse owner and so forth, and they looked suitably impressed. He said that when he read the report he rang up Mr Whitmore, the City editor, (for whom readers of Volume I may remember that I appeared in the Bank Rate Tribunal), who said that the report must have come from 'one of the crime boys'.

Now this was the plaintiff's bull point. It certainly looked as though the police had told the newspaper about the investigation. And so to

* Bolton is notoriously a marginal seat and nothing turned on the fact that he had lost Bolton.

do might well be a breach of the Official Secrets Act. And that would be quite contrary to the normal behaviour of one of the most respectable of all British newspapers, (the only newspaper I saw when I went to Buckingham Palace to be knighted) *The Daily Telegraph.* 'So let's sock 'em for that, boys.' Buster Milmo didn't actually say this, but that was the message. Nor did he go on to say that 'all the shares in the newspaper are owned by one family, and just think before you decide what damages, if any, to award.'

Mr Lewis ducked all the questions I put and when I sat down I thought that I had demonstrated that he was 'not the sort of man you would ask to dinner' (as a politician, who later became one of the great man's cabinet colleagues, once said to me of Winston Churchill when he was out in the wilderness.)

At no time, said he, was there an investigation into his company's affairs. So I read him a letter from the Commissioner of Police to the Company in August 1960 which referred to 'investigations which have been carried out by the Metropolitan and City Fraud Department' ! and added, 'I have to inform you that after careful consideration of the facts and information available, it is not proposed that any criminal proceedings should be instituted by the police as a result of such investigations.'

Then he said that he agreed that there had been an inquiry 'of a sort'.

I had a chance to put forward our views in my final speech, and pointed out that on Christmas Eve, the day after the alleged libel, the newspaper had printed a statement by Mr Lewis expressing his views of the facts, and I also told the jury that tomorrow the whole matter was going to be heard all over again because Mr Lewis and the company were then to go into battle against the *Daily Mail* (who also, perhaps foolishly, had engaged my services).

Buster followed and said that we had never published Mr Lewis's clearance from the police.

I felt that if we had, we should have been shot for digging up a long dead scandal and he would have been 'asking for more'.

I must say that I am glad that I was not in the Judge's shoes. He did it beautifully as he always does. But the public hatred of the press calls for a firm hand, and these twelve gentlemen got out of hand.

After an absence of an hour and fifty-five minutes, the jury returned and asked for evidence of movements of Rubber Improvement Ltd's share values for the ten days following the publication of the report complained of. Salmon J. said, impassively, that neither side had called evidence on the matter.

Those chosen representatives of democracy returned after twenty minutes and said :

For Mr Lewis	£25,000
For Rubber Improvements Ltd.	75,000
	£100,000

After the laughter and tears had subsided, His Lordship was informed that a sum of 250 guineas had been paid into court in each action, and he granted a stay of execution for 28 days, pending a possible appeal, on payment into court within ten days of £5,000 in respect of each plaintiff.

I offered the plaintiff's solicitor, who was the dear fellow who had sent me the hock after I had got Mr Meek out of trouble, a reasonable sum to settle the matter, but no. We had now to take on Mr L and his company again, for the *Daily Mail* who had said almost exactly the same thing.

Earlier on, many of my friends in the House of Commons had said that they would be delighted to come and say what they thought about the plaintiff. But, oddly enough, when the case became imminent (or 'eminent' as a clerk of mine used to say) they found that their commitments made it impossible for them to assist.

Milmo told them all about the livery companies and the racehorses. This time he was also a breeder of racehorses, and we heard about the boxing as well.

The opposing team was the same, but I had David Hirst as my junior.

The opening address was emotional. Apart from the racehorses we naturally heard that in the *Telegraph* action the plea for the defence in mitigation of damages was that there was a claim in respect of almost exactly the same thing against the *Daily Mail*.

And he said, as he was quite entitled to do (although he might have urged them not to be silly) that yesterday's jury, having had directions from His Lordship to take today's claim into account, had awarded £25,000 to Mr Lewis, and £75,000 to the company.

He then said that that was a lot of money but that the *Mail* had offended in ways where the *Telegraph* had not erred.

Mr Lewis went into bat. He told us that the letter of the Commissioner of Police, which I have mentioned already, was impertinent.

I asked him if, by being awarded £25,000 yesterday in respect of almost identical words, his character had been vindicated.

He said, 'No'. But he thought that the publication of his triumph had gone some way towards vindication.

I said, 'To get £25,000 free of tax you would have to earn £170,000?'

A.　I suppose your calculation would be right.

Q.　And a company would have to earn £162,000 to get £75,000 free of tax. Are you telling the jury you want more?

A.　Oh yes. I don't want another penny for myself personally, other than the costs of this action. In so far as my company is concerned, I want them to have something for that wicked libel on your part.

Q.　What proportion of the shares is controlled by you or your family?

A.　Twenty five or thirty percent.

Q.　You have effective control although not 51%?

A.　It is a family concern.

After much further cross-examination, the Judge intervened: 'I would like to hear counsel's views as to the effect of Mr Lewis's answer that he is prepared to accept an apology upon payment of his costs, and will ask for no damages for himself.'

I said that my newspaper would pay his costs and place in the front page of the *Daily Mail* tomorrow an apology which would make it clear that while they considered that they had never alleged fraud against the plaintiff, they apologised profoundly if that was the meaning of the words.

The Judge said that it was rather an unusual situation.

But Mr Milmo said that Mr Lewis's offer was conditional upon his company being awarded adequate damages.

And the case had to go on. The jury gave Mr Lewis, who didn't want anything if his company got adequate damages, £17,000 and his company £100,000!

When we took evidence before the Committee on Defamation Mr

Goldsworthy for the High Court Journalists' Association referred to this award as 'copycat damages'. An admirably succinct comment, I thought.

The jury had clearly not listened to the evidence or the cross-examination, but had heard the information in the opening speech as to the amount awarded in the *Telegraph* case, if they hadn't read it in the newspapers, and decided to punish the *Daily Mail* in the same way, but a little more so.

I cannot help thinking that a judge alone would have awarded a reasonable sum and that the unbelievably expensive bout of litigation which followed would have been avoided.

The appeals were heard together, which was satisfactory to me, as it meant that I was paid twice for arguing the appeal once. Seven months had passed since the award of the £217,000 damages, during which time, perhaps not surprisingly, no newspaper had contested a libel action in London.

The appeal lasted for many days at the end of which the court was unanimous that there must be a new trial in both cases. The appeals were allowed with costs against the plaintiffs. Lord Pearce gave the leading judgment which interested readers can find in the Law Reports.

The damages were so large that no reasonable jury could have given them without taking into account something which they were bound to exclude from their consideration and they were out of all proportion to the facts of the case. The Judge had been extremely fair in his conduct of the trial but he ought to have acceded to the defendants' submission that the innuendo ought not to be left to the jury. When words with a precise and well-known meaning were used without the addition of any expression which could impart some other flavour to them, it was not fair to twist them from their normal sense. The announcement that A was charged with murder could not of itself mean that he was guilty of murder. So much the more so, the announcement that the police were making inquiries about him in connection with a murder could not of itself mean that he was guilty of murder.

Mr Lewis went to the Lords. I rather think that the company had gone into liquidation by then. He managed to persuade Lord Morris of Borth-y-Gest that the Judge had not misdirected the jury. The other four Law Lords, led by Lord Reid, disagreed with Lord Morris of Borth-y-Gest on that point, and all five agreed that the damages were excessive and that there must be new trials, the plaintiffs to pay the costs of the newspapers in the Court of Appeal and the House of Lords, the costs of the abortive trials to abide the result of the new trial.

Lord Reid also added some remarks about tax which supported an argument of my junior, Hugh Davidson, for *The Daily Telegraph,* which David Hirst and I had declined to argue. How wrong we were is clear when succinctly stated by Lord Reid who pointed out that a company could not be injured in its feelings but only in its pocket. Its reputation could be injured by a libel but that injury must sound in money. The injury need not necessarily be confined to loss of income. Its goodwill might be injured. But insofar as the company established that the libel had, or had probably, diminished its profits the question of tax was relevant.

A jury ought to be directed, he continued, to the effect that if they thought that the plaintiff company had proved that it had suffered or would suffer a loss of profit as a result of the libel, they must bear in mind that the company would have had to pay income tax at the standard rate of that profit if it had been earned, and would only have been entitled to keep the balance, and in assessing damages the jury ought not to have taken into account the whole of that profit but should make allowance for the obligation to pay tax out of it.

The position, he concluded, with regard to an individual plaintiff was rather different. He might be entitled to very substantial damages although his income had not been affected by the libel. But if he did attempt to prove loss of income as a result of the libel, a similar direction should be given to the jury and it might be necessary to mention surtax as well as income tax.

I apologise to anyone who has found the last two or three pages rather hard going. I can only say that I find them absolutely fascinating. I wish I could have been there to hear the speeches. As it was, I had to read them in bed at Gloucester where I was trying some divorce cases which were of great importance to the parties but of no conceivable interest to anyone else.

The new trials never came on and the newspapers, flushed with triumph, settled the actions without the advice of counsel. So I have never known what were the terms.

Lewis, I think, is dead now. At any rate he is no longer in the public eye. He was a genial person, and although I did not care for him, he was never in any way discourteous, and appreciated that it was my job to cross-examine and to argue forcibly against his interests. After I became a judge he came into my court to listen on several occasions, always with a female companion.

CHAPTER THIRTEEN

One of the Faceless Fifty-three

Three years before this, while the jury were out in Lord Keyes's case, in which it was fairly clear that a very large sum of money was going to be awarded, someone I knew very well came up to me and asked me if I would accept a judgeship if I were offered one.

I had sufficient sense to say that I couldn't imagine that anyone would ever make such an offer, as I was so newly in silk, and so old. To have said anything else would have been a great mistake for it would have sounded as though I were getting above myself, and my answer would have been all round the Temple, which is always a hive of gossip, in five minutes.

I treated it as a joke and reported it to Bridget as such. That was not clever, for she took it very seriously. In vain did I point out that there were a great many silks who were years senior to me in silk and years younger in age. To pass over any of them in favour of me would be very unfair to them unless they had blotted their copy books and as far as I knew none of them had. That was not well received; she said that the fact was that I was not in with 'the right people' (whoever they might have been) and that my overwhelming claims were likely to be overlooked. And she said that it was scandalous.

After a week or two, during which it was agreed that the whole matter must be kept a CGS (closely guarded secret) from Papa, Heaven only knows why, she turned her interests to the approaching visit to Mr Finkelbaum.

Then one of the newspapers in a gossip column told the world that the maximum number of High Court puisne judges was to be increased from 48 to 53 and speculated about the new names.

> Possible names include Mr Neville Faulks, Recorder of Norwich; Mr Stanley Rees; Mr D. J. Brabin who is on the Northern Circuit; Mr T. G. Roche, Recorder of Worcester; Mr Herbert Malone; Mr J. G. S. Hobson, Recorder of Northampton; and Mr Neil Lawson. All are QCs.

When she saw that, Bridget demonstrated that she had crossed the floor. With the most touching loyalty she now declared that it would be monstrous for me to abandon my position as one of the leading advocates of the day to become what she called 'one of the faceless 53'. It wasn't much use to point out that, after sixty, one's faculties are not what they were, and that there was nothing more pathetic than to soldier on as a has-been instead of 'getting your bottom on the Consolidated Fund', for she appeared to believe that I should do a Beyfus and occupy a leading position until I was seventy-five.

It was all very sweet but rather unreal. As if I could have continued to commute up to that age. When in fact I gave it up at the age of sixty-three I had had enough, and today I should find it impossible.

The columnist was fairly well informed. Stanley Rees, who retired late in 1977 on the same day as I did, and walks innumerable miles for fun, is older than I am and was senior in silk and quite rightly was appointed before me; and so was Danny Brabin who was the best company of anyone I knew, and how he did it as a teetotaller is amazing; we were all desolated when he died in September 1975, at the early age of sixty-two. Tom Roche retired from the Bar very prosperous indeed; Herbert Malone was an odd selection, for he became a Stipendiary Magistrate, and did not occupy that position for very long; poor John Hobson became Attorney-General and died young; and Neil Lawson left the Bar to become a Law Commissioner and emerged from that position later to take his proper place on the Bench.

It is very difficult for journalists to gauge accurately what is going through the Lord Chancellor's mind or those of his advisers. Far the best article I read on this perennially interesting topic was signed 'Pendennis' and appeared in *The Observer* on 6th November 1960, a year after the Keyes trial when I had been in silk for eighteen months. It was so well informed that I felt that it must have been written by a member of the Bar. It mentioned most of the silks who were in fact promoted, but in the course of his entertaining article the writer mentioned a number of others as well who did not arrive on the Bench, although at the time they might well have been expected to do so.

At the top of the article there were a dozen photographs. Four of them became High Court Judges and Gerald Gardiner, a political appointment, became Lord Chancellor. A number of others may have refused office: I don't know. I certainly suspect that Milner Holland refused it, and Geoffrey Lawrence refused it once, but the process of selection is a mystery, which I think is a good thing.

A certain amount of doubt about the future keeps us all on our toes. I remember poor Hylton saying, when I congratulated him on being about to be appointed Speaker, 'I don't know – you know where you are going.'

And as a little boy of twenty-seven or so, before the war, I was amazed at a house-party to be told by Mrs Addie Cohen as she then was, 'Fergus is next and then it is our turn.' She was quite right and they advanced one after the other in ordered steps, until I once found myself addressing both Lord Morton of Henryton and Lord Cohen in the Lords, when they both had been recalled from retirement. Perhaps as the Chancery Bar is so much smaller the hierarchy or pecking order is that much more obvious. The *Observer* article was only dealing with advocates who were more in the public eye.

The particular weekend house-party was also graced by Sir Wilfred and Lady Greene. He had not yet become Master of the Rolls. 'You know, my boy', said Sir Wilfred, 'I was sitting quietly at Monte Carlo with a glass of champagne in my hand, ready to relax at last after being appellant in the last five cases in the Privy Council, when I got a telegram. It asked me to go direct to the Court of Appeal. I couldn't refuse, could I? But I don't know how many years it's going to take me to sort out my income tax and surtax. They really ought to give you some warning, don't you think?'

I wasn't used to hobnobbing with the great, and made some suitably acquiescent noises, but I have never forgotten the conversation.

In those days, and mercifully in my day, any money which was paid to you by way of fees, after you had left the Bar and had become one of Her Majesty's Judges, did not attract tax. When you became a judge, you sacrificed in most cases a good income for a reasonable income with longer holidays and a pension, and, if you knew or guessed that preferment was likely, you could provide yourself with a cushion against the tax problem arising from your sudden fall in income by not calling in the money owed to you too promptly. But for someone who was caught unexpectedly, like Wilfred Greene, it cannot have been amusing. Gilbert Paull is another. He was appointed at the age of sixty in the middle of a case in which I was against him, led by Sir Lionel Heald. It was in January; he didn't expect it: he had made up his books, being a meticulous fellow, at Christmas: a shame. Nowadays the appointees have to pay tax and surtax on their fees paid after their preferment as well as before. Many of them must be a trifle pushed for tax for years afterwards. I feel that this fact may in time dilute the quality of the High Court Bench.

Those who know what is or may be coming to them are those who are sent out as commissioners or, as it is often called, 'on sale or return'. One of our most respected judges was sent out in this way three times before he was appointed. It is true that, owing to extraneous circumstances and through no fault of his, he was not as busy as he deserved to be at the time, but to have suffered so would have been murder to a man with a fashionable practice.

Not every judge has to submit himself to this test. It may be that a judge dies or suddenly retires and a replacement is called for immediately, or it may be that an Act of Parliament is passed which calls for more judges. But the normal thing is that the Lord Chancellor's Department notes that old So-and-So isn't very well, or that old This-and-That is well known to wish to retire and will have done his fifteen years and qualified for his pension in another six months. Then the 'list' is consulted and the man at the top is sent out as a commissioner and thrown into the swimming pool. Many get to the other end but a surprising number seem to founder, and that of course is not a very good advertisement for them thereafter. And, if you do not emerge successfully at the other end, it can, if you were a busy man, be a very expensive immersion. I talk about the 'list', and I am sure that there must be one, but I have no proof.

In the spring of 1962, when for the first and only time someone had been appointed to the Bench who had been given silk after me, leaving Bridget to say so touchingly that it was a great shame that I had been passed over, and also that it would be a scandal if I accepted the judgeship that I had not been offered, I had a summons to see the Attorney-General.

I went across the Strand to see him. He invited me to sit down and said with the usual Manningham-Buller directness :

'Do you want to be a judge?'

I said, 'Yes' (suppressing my instinctive reply, 'But not yet', for after all I was fifty-four and the chance might not come again).

'Well, now's your chance,' he said, and proceeded to tell me that I was to be sent 'on sale or return' to Winchester for a couple of months in the summer. I wasn't pleased, as we were living beyond our means as usual, and I had just accepted the brief in the Restrictive Practices Court for the book trade, the only one that seemed to have a hope of success. I have always loved books and it would have been tremendous fun as well as helping with the overdraft.

I kept quiet and received a very helpful lecture. I can't remember it all, although 'Don't get drunk in the lodgings' sticks most firmly in my mind. He mentioned no names but mentioned four anonymous characters who had blotted their copybooks in different ways and would never be sent out as commissioners again.

It was all very alarming, and I wondered if I had a reputation for being intemperate, but it was a challenge and when I returned to June Farm and reported it in that light, there was the volte face that I had anticipated, and it was decided that at all costs I must survive the test.

There followed a letter from the Clerk to the Crown in Chancery, Sir George Coldstream, which I think I may quote although I suppose that he has the coypright :

> House of Lords,
> S.W.1.
> 25th May 1962.

Dear Faulks,

The Lord Chancellor asks me to enquire whether you would be prepared to take a long fraud case as a Commissioner of Assize at Winchester at the beginning of the Summer Term, starting there on 19th June. The Lord Chief Justice reports that it is impossible for him to spare a Judge to take this long case which is estimated to last some four weeks, as Marshall J. is still ill and there are problems on the North Eastern Circuit too.

Commission Day at Winchester is not until 9th July, but arrangements have been made for a Commissioner to take this long case at Winchester on 19th June in the hope that it can be finished before Havers and MacKenna, JJ. arrive at Winchester on 9th July.

The Lord Chancellor realises that your commitments elsewhere may make it difficult for you to accept his invitation, but he would be glad if you are able to accept it. [The Lord Chancellor, be it remembered, didn't even know me by sight. N.F.]

If you would prefer to discuss the situation with me rather than to write, do please ring me up here on Monday and we will arrange a meeting.

> Yours sincerely,
> (Signed) George Coldstream

I regarded this courteously-worded invitation as an order, and I am sure I was right. Disobedience would have made a judgeship out of the question. No one had been known to refuse such an invitation with impunity, and although it was obviously going to cost me a lot of money, I accepted without consulting Bridget who, I knew, would have been opposed. I merely told her that I had been drafted without showing her the letter. She believed me and I felt bad about it.

Then there arrived a document signed by the Monarch in her own hand, reading :–

Summer Assizes 1962

Let the name of Neville Major Ginner Faulks, Esquire MBE, TD, Honorary Lieutenant Colonel in Our Army, one of Our Counsel learned in the Law, be added to the judges who go the Western Circuit.

Bridget was very impressed by the 'Elizabeth R' and, upon my remarking how dreadfully boring it must be for the Queen to have to sign unimportant papers of that kind, she rounded on me and said it was very important and a great honour and so forth. No further opposition.

When I said that I knew that the job was going to cost me a lot of money, what I meant was this. You get substantially the same allowance whether you are alone or one of four judges at a Judge's Lodgings. Out of the allowance you have to pay the large staff and feed the good ladies who come in daily to help with the cleaning and so forth. You also have to do a great deal of entertaining in repayment of the abundant hospitality which you receive. If you are alone you haven't a hope of breaking even. Meanwhile, that lovely books brief had gone to Harry Fisher (later Mr Justice Fisher) who won the case.

I took the view, rightly as it turned out, that the High Sheriff, the Lord Lieutenant, the Mayor of Winchester, the Green Jackets, the Hampshire Law Society, and the police would not bother to entertain a mere little Commissioner of Assize and would save up the junketings for the arrival of the genuine judges on 9th July. Obviously, it would be presumptuous of me 'on sale or return' to do any entertaining on my own.

So I went to see Lord Parker the Lord Chief Justice, familiarly known as 'Hubert' to everyone except me. I don't hold with addressing

people by their Christian names if they are a number of years older
than I am, unless they invite me to do so. I was out on circuit many
times with the late Mr Justice Barry but I never called him Patrick.
Dear old Bill Gorman once said to me, 'Don't keep on calling me
Senior Judge' to which I replied, 'Well, what would you prefer?'

He said, 'Bill', and Bill it was thereafter, but he was nearly twenty
years older than I was and although we were technically brethren
I regarded him more as an uncle. Some young Benchers used to call
poor Lord Goddard, 'Rayner', when he was approaching ninety. I
thought it insufferable familiarity, and I never called him anything
but 'Lord Goddard' and he never called me anything but 'Forks'.

I was allowed to see Lord Parker of Waddington for a minute
before he went into court, and said that I was sorry to bother him but
I was in need of some sartorial advice. I said that although I was
going to be alone and would have no occasion to entertain, I had been
told that I should be expected to put on a dinner jacket every night.
Was that correct?

'Well, you must keep up some sort of state, mustn't you?' was the
reply, and I left the presence somewhat chastened. Actually I
alternated between a dinner-jacket and a rather senior ruby smoking
jacket which Bridget had bought me at Liberty's and which I have
now grown too fat to wear and have had to give away.

When I got to Winchester I was enchanted. The lodgings are too
small for a lot of judges but they are ideal for one or two. When I was
called to the Bar I didn't know any judges and accordingly I had
never been a Judge's Marshal, or even entered a Judges' Lodgings
except on rare occasions when I had been asked to luncheon. This
was because I was seldom out of London. I had once been to a
cocktail party at Leeds, once to luncheon at Maidstone and once to
luncheon at Chelmsford, seeing nothing but the dining-room and the
lavatory.

So Winchester was a treat. The lodgings are in the Close opposite
the Deanery, and are easily recognisable because when the judges, or
even a commissioner, are there, the Union Jack flies from the flagstaff.
There is that glorious cathedral ahead with a sung evensong most
days, although I have never thought the choir to be as good as at
Worcester, Gloucester or Exeter. I may be unfair in saying that for it
depends on the time of year that one goes. Obviously, if one goes at
the beginning of the school year, (and the boys come from the Pilgrims'

School in the close just opposite the second judge's bedroom) you don't get such good singing as you do when the Precentor has been at them for some time. I have noticed this in the Temple too. The boys there come from the City of London School and they all adore Dr Thalben-Ball whose fiftieth year as choirmaster we celebrated with a great dinner, and their singing improves wonderfully as the months pass.

I hope that George Thalben-Ball made a great deal of money out of 'Oh for the wings of a dove' and 'Hear my prayer', the record which was so popular in my youth, with the boy soprano who not long ago resigned as the leading baritone in the choir. He certainly ought to have done, as he gave so much pleasure to so many.

I am no descriptive writer and will only say that at Winchester a before-breakfast walk to St Cross and back through the meadows was a life-saver, for to be all alone with a long fraud case is a somewhat depressing experience.

The case itself could not have been more suitably chosen for me, if I had to do crime. For it was all about a complicated swindle concerning motor-cars, and might just as well have been presented by the Board of Trade as prosecutors, instead of the Director of Public Prosecutions. Most of the silks on the Western Circuit were in it and some of them, in a very civilised way, persuaded their clients to plead 'guilty'. I was left with only two trials to deal with, each of which took three or four days only. The jury convicted in each case, the criminals were small fry and I gave them eighteen months or two years. On the other hand, one of the characters who, with his wife, had pleaded 'guilty' was, I thought, a bad man. It obviously wouldn't be very clever to be upset in the Court of Criminal Appeal when you were only pretending to be a judge, but I felt that I had to do what I thought right rather than play safe. I gave him ten years, ticked his wife off, and sent her home to look after her baby who would otherwise have had to be 'taken into care'.

Dear me, I thought, they are bound to say it was too severe as well as lop-sided. And the late Cyril Harvey QC bounced off happily to the CCA. He was astounded, but not more than was I, when the three wise men said that it was a very proper sentence and that it was high time that a stop was put to this sort of thing. The appeal was dismissed.

So the long case turned out not too long, and I was ready to go home. But the Clerk of Assize was much too smart for me. My name had been added to the list of the judges who 'go the Western Circuit', and, technically, I was not appointed to deal with this one case alone. There was another much longer case which it was hoped that I would take as I was now free.

I had no alternative, and we went on and on for weeks. When their Lordships, who had now grown to three with the addition of Mr Justice Cairns, as he then was, arrived, they found me still plodding on. I was sent upstairs to what must have been the second housemaid's bedroom, but I did not worry, although it would not have been amusing if I had had my wife with me. She and Papa came to luncheon once which they enjoyed. It was only an hour and a half from June Farm and if I had to go as commissioner I couldn't have chosen a better place. The point about Papa was that although he looked likely to live more or less for ever, one never knew, and he ought not to be left. The cook and the devoted Mrs Hamilton came to help us daily, as did Taylor the gardener, and my daughter Judith was a day girl at Micklefield School, Reigate. There was no question therefore of Bridget coming with me and it was a lonely life.

Mindful of Reggie Manningham-Buller's Polonius-like precepts, I played the near teetotaller, having one glass of sherry before dinner and that was that. I also told the housekeeper, an elderly lady called Mrs Mould, that I wasn't particular about my food. That was very well received, as she said that there had been some trouble about engaging the cook whom she had intended to get for me, and would I mind very much if she gave one of her girls, who was very promising, the chance to cook for me, as after all she could only learn by experience. I was all smiles and agreed.

The girl, whom I never saw, for I was not sufficiently sure of myself to venture into the kitchen, turned out to be an adequate 'good plain cook', although far below the standard of the lady who reigns there today, and I was quite satisfied.

When the judges arrived, Mrs Mould was heard to say that 'the Commissioner has very simple tastes', and the old Adam inside me roared with laughter.

While we were at Winchester came the night of the Long Knives when Mr Macmillan changed his cabinet and offered the Attorney-General the post of Lord Chancellor. Like a sensible fellow he accepted and took the title of Lord Dilhorne. Kilmuir having gone, I felt a bit happier about the future. I used to go home for the weekends and for one of them we were asked to stay with Lord Rothermere who was then unmarried. He was hospitality itself, but for some reason was greatly entertained by Reggie Manningham-Buller's new title which he pronounced incorrectly.

I am fairly sure that these cabinet changes occurred while we were at Winchester because I remember vividly a discussion in the sitting-room about the new Law Officer. The others were baffled except for a half-hearted suggestion of Charles Doughty, and I made so bold as to say that of course the new Solicitor-General would be Peter Rawlinson. This occasioned some surprise, but when I audaciously offered to bet that I was right, nothing more was said. I was right and I don't suppose that the senior judge could possibly have contemplated that in ten years time his own child would be Solicitor-General. He lived to see that, but died in 1977, greatly lamented, before Sir Michael Havers became a Privy Councillor.

Winchester is a marvellous place to go to on circuit provided that there are not too many wives, marshals, clerks and what have you, when the lodgings are not big enough. But in that July they put on a 'Son et Lumière' in the Cathedral, with Donald Wolfit doing the commentary, which was really moving. The evening was warm and all the recording instruments performed well and you could envisage King Canute clattering up the nave without difficulty. It was a Friday night when we went and Bridget and I went home thereafter. I had by now learned that if I left home at half-past eight on Monday morning I could be in court on time, so that I actually had three nights at home each week, although I was theoretically on the Western Circuit.

Mr Justice Havers was so kind to me. I asked him about what to say in my summing up. He said that as the case had been going on for weeks I must start by being a little pompous and offering the jury the thanks of the county and observing that it had been plain to me that they had been paying the greatest attention to the matter even in its most technical and uninteresting parts, and that I at any rate would always be grateful for having been afforded such assistance etc. Five minutes of that, he said, and you'll be all right.

This experienced judge certainly knew what he was about. I did as he told me, and they all appeared to listen to my lengthy summing up with enthusiasm. The prosecution who could have called one of the accused to 'shop' all the others failed for reasons which I could not understand, to do so, and all the accused were found 'not guilty'.

Then came the Long Vacation. Although we did not know it, it was to be our last family holiday together. We parked Papa, now aged eighty-six, with one of my sisters and went off to the Reina Cristina at Algeciras. I had been there twice before the war, going out to Gibraltar and back in the old *Rawalpindi*. This time Bridget, Esmond, Judith and I went by air, and Nigel who was twenty-one and just down from Cambridge, came by car from Portugal with his friend Richard Hughes. He was the only one child to have left school and we had given him a tiny Renault for his birthday.

It was a good holiday, as we had a pleasantly large sitting-room in our suite and could get away from everyone if we wished. This was necessary, as the place was not as restful as in the old days, due to the advent of the motor coach. But, although I incurred a little temporary unpopularity by refusing to accompany the rest of the party to a bull fight, I think they all enjoyed themselves. It turned out to be a very Norwich occasion. Mr Justice Havers, who was a widower, was a Norfolk man and he was there. So was his son Michael and his family, and so too Oliver Prior and his. Oliver was the Clerk of the Peace at Norwich, and the local Pooh-Bah, Michael was one day to be the last Recorder of Norwich before the Beeching Report was implemented, and I was the then Recorder.

I succeeded Fred Beney QC, who ought to have been a judge, and was followed by my old friend Colin Duncan QC, who was too old to be a judge, and at the moment it looks as though Sir Michael Havers has adopted a political career and may not want to be a judge. Before Fred there was an old fellow called Sir Ellis Hume-Williams QC who was Recorder for a very long time and was a popular figure, although it is said that he was generally to be found in the Carlton Club on the first day of Quarter Sessions, having overlooked the appointment. So although it was such a desirable recordership in such a beautiful cathedral city, I seem to have been the only recorder within living memory to have become a judge.

Richard and Nigel played interminable games of ping-pong by the sea at Tavira Point and we had some foot-wearing games of lawn tennis on the concrete tennis-court, but it wasn't a very energetic holiday.

In 1974, my two sons set out, aged thirty-three and twenty-eight respectively, to walk the Pennine Way from Edale in Derbyshire, where Elizabeth spent much of her childhood with her grandmother, who was one of seventeen children and lived to ninety-eight, to Hexham in Northumberland, near to which Esmond lives. I told them that they wanted their heads examined, but they knew best, and enjoyed an experience which would have been far too energetic for me.

Before I had left England I had had another letter from the Lord Chancellor on an entirely different subject which contained what I thought to be a very significant sentence, 'I am grateful to you for helping us out at Winchester and I have heard very favourable comments.'

I had shown it to Bridget and indicated that I was of the opinion that I knew the Lord Chancellor too well to believe that he would be leading me up the garden path. She took it well enough when I pointed out that the Conservative Macmillan administration was not expected to last very long, that Gerald Gardiner, who would be unpredictable, was likely to be the next Lord Chancellor, and that the higher judiciary appeared to be in uniformly robust health and unlikely to supply a vacancy. I merely told my clerk that I had received a kind letter from the Lord Chancellor's office, and he drew his own conclusions and did not hurry to send out the fee notes.

I ought to say that Gerald Gardiner made an admirable and dignified Lord Chancellor and that his appointments were unimpeachable and in no manner 'way out', as had been feared in some quarters. I think that he was lonely in his job, and I remember his coming to luncheon in 1970, when his period of office was over, and saying that he felt like a schoolboy loose for the holidays. 'Now at last someone will speak to me again,' he said. He set up the Law Commission, which has been of undeniable value, and has furthered his 'recreation', always described in *Who's Who* as 'law reform'. The late Mr Justice Howard who had been a Conservative Member of Parliament always used to refer to him as 'that dangerous Socialist fanatic.'

When the autumn came Nigel went off to be a pupil in Company chambers and the other children went back to school. Papa practically lived in the television room smoking St Bruno Rough Cut, which would have been too much for most people half a century younger, and the work came pouring in.

CHAPTER FOURTEEN

Local Boy Makes Good

I had a case which started on 19th November 1962 and which lasted for a number of days, in which I was appearing for C. T. Bowring & Co. Ltd., immensely important people in the shipping and insurance world. Once more the case had originally gone to Gardiner, but I had had the brief in the Long Vacation, so that his clerk had thrown it back into the pool early enough for the clients to get a second string who had thoroughly familiarised himself with the facts and law.

Ashe Lincoln QC was against me, for whom I had recently appeared and obtained damages against David Daniels. As I remember it, the case concerned whether or not the plaintiff should have been made a 'name' at Lloyds. He was apparently intensely suspicious of my clients and the most ludicrous situation arose when it was found that the case was down for hearing before Mr Justice (now Lord Justice) Megaw. Somehow or other it was discovered that John Megaw had his robes insured with Bowrings and he was objected to as a tribunal : I can only imagine it was because it was thought that he would be likely to be biassed as a consequence. It didn't help the plaintiff very much as we had Mr Justice Thompson who had been against me in *Rookes* v *Barnard*. He dealt with the matter in a thoroughly commonsense manner.

When eventually Ashe Lincoln stood up to say that, in the circumstances and the way in which the evidence stood, the plaintiff agreed to submit to judgment and costs, and to abandon all claims of any kind against Bowrings, their servants or agents, John Thompson said that it was a very proper decision which merely anticipated the conclusion to which he would inevitably have been driven.

When I add that he also stated that it was manifest that the plaintiff himself did not think that the allegations he had made could be substantiated against my clients, it was clear that we hadn't done too badly.

So the clients decided to give me a treat, two treats to be exact. One, I was to have an interview with the great panjandrum of Bowrings, the ruling member of the family for the time being; and two, I was to see their brand new computer near the Tower of London.

As I have said, I never approved of the practice of having a meal with the clients, but these people were representatives of a vast company rather than individual clients, and they were so charming that it was impossible to decline their invitation. During the case they had booked a table every day at a restaurant in Bush House, and it was the greatest fun, as there was no strain on me, the case being one that it was almost impossible to lose. A very large team used to appear including Cosmo Crawley, the rackets player, and a Bowring who had had a son who had been captain of rugger at Uppingham. There was much laughter.

The treat didn't work out in the same way. I was kept waiting for quite a time before I was shown into the presence. It was made quite plain that the great man, whom I had not the slightest desire to see, and of whose existence I was unaware, was very busy indeed. I have never been so heavily patronised in my life; he was Hamlet and I was the little Player King. I was polite and humble, eventually extricated myself, and went off to luncheon with the clients before the second part of the treat.

I think that his initials began with N, but I may be wrong. He is not in *Who's Who* and perhaps he is no more. Probably it was only that, as they used to say of me in my school reports, 'he has an unfortunate manner'.

I was never to see the computer, for as I was sitting down to deal with a superb luncheon in an underground cave in the City, with a good deal of alcohol being triumphantly consumed, I was told that I was wanted on the telephone. I imagined that it would be my clerk, for no one else could possibly have traced me, and I wasn't pleased, because I had thought that for once I was actually to have the afternoon off, the opposition having collapsed so unexpectedly in the morning. But it was official. Could I find it convenient to see the Lord Chancellor at three o'clock? 'Yes sir, yes sir, three bags full', and I said goodbye to my kind hosts whom I have never seen since, goodbye to their computer, and took a taxi to the House of Lords.

At this time there was another bonanza coming up for the Bar at which I was to be the principal beneficiary. It was called 'The Vassall Tribunal'. This man was a traitor, who is now out of prison, and I hope that he went in for long enough to enable me to escape punishment under the Rehabilitation of Offenders Act for telling truthfully that he was a traitor.

The newspapers had gone to town on this very newsworthy item, and some of them were possibly in trouble. Everyone was very excited, and I had read up all the laws of the various States of America, where in some States, a journalist is entitled to put his hand on his heart, and decline to reveal the source of his information (which would be very helpful if he were himself the source of his own information), and get away with it on grounds of privilege. I was looking forward to this tribunal enormously. It would have been absolutely up my street, and there were a large number of briefs which I had accepted.

When the Chancellor offered me a judgeship, he said, 'It won't be what you want : it will have to be in the Divorce Division; Collingwood is too ill to go on; there may not be another vacancy while I'm Chancellor and you'll be a mug if you don't take it.'

I wanted to be a judge and knew that Bridget, whom I thought I could persuade, didn't. I wanted to be 'local boy made good', but I wanted to keep my children in bread and boots for as long as I could, and the appointment would mean a substantial drop in income. So I asked if I could be appointed after the end of the Vassall Tribunal. Charming but inflexible, he said, 'No'. I gave in. He gave me until 10th January 1963 when I should be sworn in. Meanwhile we had the 'Closely Guarded Secret'. I wasn't allowed to tell my clerk, I had to swear my poor wife to secrecy, and I had to continue accepting briefs for the Vassall Tribunal (the *Daily Telegraph* for instance) and to go on having desperately important consultations when I knew that I should not be there to open on the night. This tremendous secrecy must be maddening to solicitors and I think to be absolutely unnecessary. Many years ago Earl Jowitt made Colin (now Lord) Pearson a judge at the *beginning* of the Long Vacation, the appointment to take effect on 1st October. How very sensible.

Having kept my well-known mouth shut for what seemed a very long time over Christmas, we had to await the announcement in *The Times* newspaper before we could speak, and then get ready to answer all the kind letters of congratulation.

My Christmas Vacation had been spent in reading, reading very carefully, *Rayden on Divorce* which I found, I am sorry to say, most

Procession at Lincoln 1972. 'If you ask me, I'd give him life'

Equestrian sports: Elizabeth and Jenny 1958

Aquatic sports at Wittenham House: Andrew and Jenny 1964

uninteresting to read as well as exceedingly awkward to hold. We had the usual houseful, and there was speculation as to what on earth I was up to with this great tome, but Bridget kept the secret and all was well.

The appointment was announced on 28th December 1962 to take effect on the resignation of Mr Justice Collingwood who was seventy-five and in ill health.

The Daily Telegraph gave me a good notice complete with not-too-flattering photographs, but then I am not photogenic. So did the Rothermere newspapers. I think that *The Times* made the announcement without comment but in a position of some prominence.

It was about half-way between their practice today and that in the preceding year when I remember opening my *Times* in bed at Norwich to see a great photograph of Stanley Rees staring at me below the announcement 'Mr Stanley Rees QC to be a High Court Judge'. An important event : My appointment was an event : today it is apparently a non-event, for the appointment appears in small print on the Court page next to that of the assistant rodent exterminator for Cumbria and similar other topical items.

Then I had to find myself some robes in order to appear in full fig to be sworn in before the Lord Chancellor. Arrangements were made for me to purchase Mr Justice Collingwood's full-bottomed wig, and his scarlet and ermine robes. This could have been better organised as I have a fat head, size $7\frac{5}{8}$, whereas his was normal or slightly smaller than normal. It also seemed that he was about three inches shorter than I was and I am only 5 ft. $10\frac{1}{2}$ ins. I suppose that I already had my breeches, silk stockings, and fancy shoes from the day that I took silk, and the rest of the paraphernalia was not too difficult to acquire. But it was a very hot and self-conscious and even more than usually red-faced character who drove down to the Lords from his chambers for the ceremony.

It was very simple. I had been told that I might take my family, and although Nigel had another engagement, Bridget, Papa, Esmond and Judith were there. I was very nervous but the Chancellor did it all as to the manner born. I was the first appointment he had made and he might have been expected to be slightly tense, but he was very charming and the family were greatly impressed. I find that I possess a very unflattering photograph of the occasion which I think must have been sent by an East Anglian newspaper, as the reading matter dwells a lot on Norwich.

So I was Mr Justice Faulks, but still Mr Faulks. Then I got a letter from Mr Macmillan's office marked 'confidential'.

Dear Mr Justice Faulks,

I write to inform you, at the Prime Minister's request, that the Queen has been pleased to approve that the Honour of Knighthood be conferred upon you on your appointment as a Judge of the High Court of Justice.

A notice to this effect will, therefore, appear in the morning papers of Thursday, January 17th.

Your sincerely,

Tim Bligh.

It didn't say *when*, and it was 'confidential' so I didn't tell Bridget and when I had to go to some City dinner to make a speech I was unable to answer any questions on the subject.

On 22nd January, however, I received another communication, this time from the Home Office. I couldn't read the signature, but it said after giving the date :

Dear Mr Justice Faulks,

I write to confirm that it would accord with the Queen's convenience to receive you, in private audience, at Buckingham Palace at 11.45 a.m. on Tuesday, 29th January in order to confer the honour of Knighthood upon you. Morning dress should be worn.

Bridget was very excited about this, but I kept wondering where I was going to park the car and what I was going to say, for I had been told that these private audiences lasted for twenty minutes. She solved the problem by telling me to leave the car in the Law Courts and take a taxi, and also by reading out of the *Daily Mail* on the morning of the occasion the information that the Queen and the Duke of Edinburgh had been the night before to see a play which we had seen the week before. It had entertained us greatly and was called *The Public Ear and the Private Eye,* or something of that kind, and featured Kenneth Williams. It would be a standby if necessary, although I had always been told that you must never initiate a conversation with Royalty. Prince Philip had, however, told me at Deal, on the only occasion that I had met him, that that was no longer the case.

I entered Buckingham Palace in some trepidation, but was most kindly looked after by some very senior sort of bear-leader who led me through a number of rooms before I was introduced to the presence. He very kindly told me how to kneel and on which knee, and what to grasp hold of in case I stumbled, and how to back out when the audience was terminated. It was all somewhat alarming but all that disappeared at once when I was inside the room. I dare say that I failed to do the right thing but there was such grace and charm that I was not made aware of it.

I suppose that the Queen had been told that I acted for a number of newspapers, for the conversation was led in that direction and we discussed the Press, and later I managed to get in the bit about the theatre which went well as the Queen said, 'And do you think he really was eating yoghurt?' We had sat in the front row of the stalls and I was able to say, deferentially but confidently, that he was. I also remembered to say 'Mam' several times in what I deemed to be appropriate places. Perhaps I over-egged the pudding but it did not seem to give offence.

I am recalling this audience after more than fifteen years, and I can remember no more for I have never kept a record of an interview and cannot be as exact as Mr Cecil King, or the late Mr Crossman. What struck me most was how much more beautiful the Queen was in real life than in most of her portraits and those dreadful stamps. No wonder she is said to have liked the first Annigoni, for it showed her as she really was.

She was going to Australia the next day and, as I saw in the Court Circular in *The Times,* she had a very full programme for my day after she had got rid of me; but it was all so pleasant and easy, and no hint that it was, as it must have been, work, and rather boring work at that.

Apart from Royal Garden Parties, the only other time that I have entered the august portals was to play lawn tennis against the Royal Household. They were not very good but it was great fun. Some days before the match I received a letter from Paddy Dunboyne who was organising it. His Lordship wished the players to know that the Royal swimming bath would be at their disposal after their exertions, *but* that it was essential that rather than soil the Royal water with their disgusting sweaty plebeian bodies it was imperative that a shower be taken before immersion, and it was optional whether another should be taken thereafter.

I had managed to persuade Paddy to let me have Barry Carter for a partner, who had been a pupil of mine and had been captain of the CULTC. The enemy couldn't take my silly spin service and he did the rest. But I was anxious to remember about that shower. I did, and was so pleased with myself that I dived immediately into the Royal bath only to discover when I got to the other end that I was stark naked. Fortunately, it appeared to be 'men only' that day.

When the Lord Chancellor told me the only job he was offering me was in the Probate, Divorce and Admiralty Division and that I shouldn't like that, he sincerely meant what he said. But while I was at Winchester I had been surveying the field with an eye to expressing a choice, if I got the chance, if and when I was offered a judgeship. The Probate, Divorce and Admiralty Division was then regarded as a sort of second eleven, and during the Presidency of the late Lord Merriman it was generally known as 'the OCTU' because judges seemed to stay there for three or four years and then be transferred to the Queen's Bench Division. In those days the QBD dealt with all the serious crime as well as all the accident cases, which make up over ninety per cent of the civil work, the odd defamation case or action for damages for breach of contract accounting for the rest. It was true that it seemed that work in the P.D. and A. could be boring, for there wasn't much P. about and the A. would be handled by Hewson J. who had been in the Merchant Navy, Karminski J., who had been in the Royal Navy during the war, or Jack Simon himself on the basis that 'if you can try anything, you can try everything', as he was wont to say, and as he has indeed demonstrated to be the case since he went to the Lords. I too was prepared to accept that the Admiralty work, where you had assessors to keep you on the right lines, was mostly a matter of trying running-down actions at sea.

But there were obvious advantages in belonging to the P.D. and A. Division. Only fourteen weeks a year away from the family, on circuit, was a tremendous consideration when Judith was twelve, and Bridget would not be able to leave her much while she was at day-school. And I had always felt that Cicero had a point when he spoke in the Pro Sestro of *otium cum dignitate,* the former noun to be taken to refer to a peaceful rather than an idle existence. At Uppingham I had thought it rather exciting when one of the older boys in Dr Taylor's form announced with great triumph that he was a hedonist, (a word he had probably learned the day before) but on reflection I had decided that what a growing boy should aim for was bags of otium coupled with a spot of the old dignitate. (I was a keen Wodehouse fan.)

As I looked round the lodgings at Winchester I had noticed that Havers J., in spite of his very great experience, became very tired in the evening and had to consult his notes now and then, and that MacKenna J. seemed somewhat bored with people falling off ladders, and had to consult his notes rather a lot, while Cairns J. (lately Lord Justice Cairns), the P.D. and A. judge, seemed very relaxed, on top of his work, and never looked at his notes at all. He had been a very distinguished commercial lawyer and had been out of the hunt for years, as the first Chairman of the Monopolies Commission, a position of some distinction. I was fairly sure that he had had even less experience of Divorce matters than had I, although I didn't like to ask him. Lady Cairns came down for a few days and seemed very relaxed also, and I made up my mind to opt for the Divorce Division. When, therefore, I took with grace the bone I was assumed not to want, I in fact accepted it with glee.

And I am still happy about it. I was a cross between a parson and a probation officer, with enough legal knowledge to enable me to make my solution acceptable. It is the least boring and sometimes the most challenging occupation offered to a humble puisne judge.

Bridget was of course correct in prophesying that in accepting a judgeship I was consigning myself to obscurity. Everybody has heard of Lord Denning, some of Lord Scarman, and a few of Mr Justice Melford Stevenson who always seems to try the most reportable cases. Some Law Lords swim temporarily into the public eye and out again as they complete the designated chore. John Donaldson has had his fill of being a public figure and, I should think, is glad to return to anonymity. But the rest are nameless, which is absolutely right. And why should I not be one of them? I had worked very hard for a very long time, others were cleverer and more ambitious, so that if I wanted a quiet time, I should not be depriving our national jurisprudence of any great contribution. She and I would see much more of each other and we could afford to continue to live at June Farm which would be a white elephant if I had to be out on circuit for two thirds of the year like the poor Q.B. judges.

Bridget seemed to take the point and accompanied me for two or three days to Gloucester on circuit. She spent the days with her friend, Mary Foster, at Cheltenham, and dined with us at night, but soon she had to go home to see Papa and Judith. By this time, we had given up living-in staff, our last 'treasure' having spent most of her time being ill and having to be visited in hospital, and we relied on daily help and the gardener.

It was at about this time that Papa gave up going to London daily, possibly because of advancing years (eighty-six) or more probably because he did not like being taken to and fetched from the station in the gardener's small car. What with Papa and fetching and carrying Judith from and to school which was done on a rota basis with another mother, Bridget could not be away for long.

However she did come. I was not the senior judge. Mr Justice Hewson, the Admiralty judge, who later retired owing to ill-health, and has since died, was my companion. He had seldom been out on circuit before, as the Admiralty work is done in London, and when I asked if my wife might come for a day or two, he said 'yes', immediately, but seemed surprised that I had bothered to ask.

There was and still is a great deal of protocol at Judges' Lodgings such as – if you ask the High Sheriff and the Lord Mayor on the same night, which precedes the other into dinner? I have known a lot of time to be spent on this conundrum and when I have interjected, 'Well, don't ask them both on the same night', I have been brushed aside as being incurably flippant again.

The position of wives was however of tremendous importance. ('Faulks', 'Yes sir', 'I should like you to write me an essay on the position of women in the time of Pericles.' 'Yes sir'.)

I went out to Gloucester shortly after my appointment simply because I was slotted into the place marked 'Collingwood' for my predecessor. But we chose our circuits for the summer at my first judge's meeting and I chose Birmingham when my turn came. It didn't sound very attractive but it was very nearly Hobson's choice. I didn't know then, but it (the Judges' Lodgings) has a first class billiards table and croquet lawn and is within walking distance of the Edgbaston Golf Club, the Priory Tennis Club and the Botanical Gardens, while there is any amount of good music to be had, apart from the joys of the Barber Art Gallery at the University, and the City of Birmingham Art Gallery itself. It became my favourite stamping ground for a number of years, and I was remarried from there in 1967.

Shortly after I had made my choice, I received a letter from Owlie Stable whom I didn't then know personally, although on my appointment I had had a charming letter from his wife, Lucie, whom I only knew by sight also. 'I shall be delighted if you will bring your wife for some or all of the duration of your stay in Birmingham.' This seemed very thoughtful but of course I was going to bring my wife. I was going on circuit, not to war. What was all this about?

I inquired of one of my friends who had been a judge for some years and was much-married. I couldn't imagine him going on circuit as a bachelor, or grass-widower, as it used to be called when I was a boy. He told me that it was an immemorial custom that the women were the guests of the judges in the lodgings and that a judge had no right to bring his wife unless the Senior Judge sent him a formal invitation, in which case she would be a guest in the house and her husband would not be allowed to pay for her keep, the cost of which would be shared among all. If you didn't get such a letter, it was too bad and you couldn't bring your wife.

I couldn't believe this, and said that the lodgings surely were not supposed to be a monastery if some elderly judges so willed. He said, 'Not a monastery, but, shall we say, an officers' mess? And it works.' I asked, 'How?' and he told me of talkative wives and those who poked their noses into the kitchen. I said that such cases must be few and far between, but he didn't agree. I said that it wasn't right that a misogynist, or someone who didn't get on with his own wife, should be entitled to deprive his juniors of their home comforts. Each of us should be entitled to bring our own wife and pay for them. This was all very amicably discussed, but he said that the rule had been in existence for far too long to admit of change.

In the event it was not until after poor Bridget's death in May, 1963, that I got to Birmingham where Lucie was with Owlie, and Pam Mocatta with Alan, and everything was very pleasant.

Later, after I remarried, I took up the cudgels again, I am happy to say, with success. Nowadays you may take your wife for 'a visit or visits', and merely should notify the Senior Judge of your intention, as a matter of courtesy. I have no doubt but that 'a visit or visits' is a form of words designed by the last ditchers to indicate that one or a succession of weekends is envisaged, but to me a 'visit' includes a stay for the whole period at the lodgings if so desired.

CHAPTER FIFTEEN

In the Midst of Life

For obvious reasons I do not wish to dwell on Bridget's death, but this account would be incomplete without a short recital of the facts. She kissed me goodbye in the morning, and I walked through the garden, past all the forget-me-nots, to the gate. I drove to the station, parked the car, and did a morning's work trying a defended divorce case. At luncheon I sat eating some cold tongue and salad and wondering how I could shorten what promised to be an interminable cross-examination, when one of my fellow benchers came in and said, 'Your clerk wants you : one of your witnesses is ill or dead or something.'

I thanked him and went out and there at the bottom of the stairs was my dear clerk, William, looking very upset. He said, 'Your sister is here', and showed me down to a committee room where Lorna and Richard, Bridget's half-brother, were standing. William tactfully left us, and Lorna told me what had happened.

It seemed that Bridget and Richard had gone shopping and, on their return, Bridget had gone into the drawing-room where Papa was smoking his pipe as usual, looking at *The Times* crosswood puzzle. She had done a couple of clues and had then been baffled. She sat down opposite him, saying that she would read the *Daily Mail*. She coughed, stood up, swayed, and was caught by Mrs Hamilton, our daily help, who had been busying herself nearby. She coughed again, collapsed, and was dead. Mrs Hamilton laid her on the ground. All this was observed by Papa, Mrs Hamilton, and Richard standing at the door, shopping-basket in hand. I suppose they sent for the doctor. I don't know.

Lorna only lived two or three miles away, and was devoted to Bridget. She brought Richard up to see me and to drive me home. I must have been slightly demented, for I insisted on going upstairs and buttonholing a very senior judge and asking him whether in the circumstances he thought that I could properly abandon my case for the afternoon. He sympathetically said that I could and that he would tell my clerk, and only then did I agree to face what was in store.

I asked to be driven to pick up my car at the station, and to be left alone to tell Judith. I found that she was playing tennis and collected her. Like a fool, I tried to break it gently much too soon. Hysterics. We were driving along a very narrow country lane emerging on to the Reigate-Dorking road. I was not altogether in control of myself. As I came out I collided with a man on a bicycle. He didn't seem hurt but the bicycle was not improved. I took him to the local garage, and gave him my name and address and £25. I have never heard of him since. Judith was whimpering away.

The house seemed empty, and Bridget was on the floor. Suddenly there seemed to be a number of people there, Dr Sheldon, Papa and all the rest of them. The doctor said that it was virus pneumonia and that he couldn't have done anything if he had been there at the time. We had a pathologist's report which didn't tell us anything. It was all very grisly.

I wore a black tie for exactly twelve months, which in most people would look absurdly ostentatious. As my professional clothes had to be sub fusc this escaped attention, except on one occasion when an acquaintance congratulated me on my meticulousness in observing Court Mourning for King Haakon of Norway.

I was a widower for four years and a bit thereafter. Not a period of much happiness, although everyone was very kind. Judith stayed with various friends for her last term at Micklefield, and Papa went off to John and Lorna while I was at Birmingham. Esmond returned to Uppingham after the funeral and Nigel to digs in London. I don't remember but presumably the 'dailies' and Taylor, the gardener, kept the house going.

When the Long Vacation came I arranged for myself and the three children to accompany Papa to the Royal Duchy Hotel at Falmouth which was owned by a company of which he was a director and in which I had some shares. Tennis, surfing, much rain and endless driving through narrow lanes.

When we got back it was time to get Judith ready to go to school at Benenden where she was due to start in September. Mercifully Miriam Odgers, to whom I owe so much, had a daughter, Charlotte, who was also going to the school at the same time, and she, Miriam, was a wonderful substitute mother. For the next four years or more I seem to have driven down to Benenden and back, about a hundred miles, every weekend when I was not on circuit, except in the holidays. But no doubt I exaggerate.

I had to go somewhere in the autumn. Leeds, I think. While I was there I had a letter from the President of the Probate Division saying that none of the judges had put their names down for the Lord Mayor's Banquet and I must consider myself a 'volunteer' to go with him. I didn't feel much like it. I hadn't volunteered as I was in mourning, quite apart from not wanting to dress up in full regalia and sit down to dinner in a full-bottomed wig. One needs a companion for such junketings. A week after I had reluctantly accepted, it was revealed that the Lord Mayor had decided to invite the judges who were attending to bring their wives. Certain of my brethren suddenly discovered that they would be able to attend after all, but it was too late. I took Anne Guest, the charming wife of Ronald Guest, who used to be in our chambers, and I like to think that we enjoyed ourselves very much.

The next time that I went to this function I was able to take Elizabeth, and she has never ceased to want to go again. I don't suppose we ever shall now. She put on all her jewellery and we sat opposite an Air Chief Marshal whose wife had also been to the bank, and they both looked superb and neither felt too ostentatiously dressed. Next on the other side was an important Soviet functionary and his delightful wife with whom we got on exceedingly well. Elizabeth persuaded the husband to put on my wig, which he enjoyed. He may have suspected that there was a tape recorder concealed within it, but if so, he did not tell us.

There was dancing, and we were quietly revolving round the floor when our friend from Moscow decided to treat it as an 'excuse me' dance, which I thought to be a bit much, although I gave way peacefully. The last I saw of him that evening was kissing Canon John (José to me when we were at Cambridge) Collins in the gentlemen's lavatory with true Oriental flamboyance. Alas for all that merriment! The only time I have seen him since was on television trying to justify the Russian rape of Czechoslovakia, and the downfall of Dubcek. Seldom have I seen a man look so frightened and unhappy.

CHAPTER SIXTEEN

Tail-end Charlie

I was sent to the first of these banquets because I was 'Tail-end Charlie', the junior judge, and I remained such for over a year. The Chancellor had been right when he said that there would not be many appointments during his term of office. It was not until a year later that Milmo J. was appointed. He must have had an enjoyable audience, in his turn, as he had been for many years standing counsel to the Jockey Club. He still hunts with the Crawley and Horsham, rising seventy while Kenneth (Lord) Diplock keeps the flag flying in Leicestershire rising seventy-one; but then he looks about fifty-five.

The result of this year as a junior judge meant that I had to be the Vacation Judge for a whole year, alternating with Eustace (now Lord Justice) Roskill, which was almost an unheard of thing, as judicial vacancies occurred normally more than once a year. This meant giving up half if not the whole of each vacation to deal with urgent matters. I rather enjoyed it however. First, it kept my mind off our domestic situation, and second, it was fun trying Chancery matters of which I had no experience at all. The Chancery Division deals with companies, bankruptcies, pollution of rivers, breaking of trusts, estate duty, death duties, and divers other matters which ordinary mortals cannot be expected to understand. It is always assumed, no doubt correctly, that the Chancery Judges are much cleverer than we are, and it is noticeable that it seems to take them longer to get to the Bench, but that once they are there they whistle up through the Court of Appeal into the Lords in very little time. However, provided counsel is competent and explains it all in words of one syllable, it is possible for us to arrive at the right solution, although not as quickly as active Chancery judges and that is an entertaining challenge. If I could have had a little time off in some other part of the year to compensate, I would have been delighted to be Vacation Judge until I retired. As this particular piece of information will not reach the office of the Lord Chancellor until after I have retired it may be wondered why I bother to state it. There may however be others younger than myself who feel the same. And I did volunteer to be the Queen's Bench Vacation Judge for 1975 to give myself a change, although I got no compensatory leave.

Since my appointment only two judges have left the Family Division for the QBD, each to be 'presiding judge' of a circuit, an expression brought in as a result of the Beeching Report. Apart from them we have had no transfers except by way of promotion to the Court of Appeal, and the day of the OCTU is over. Recent legislation has given us the Wards of Court which had been, illogically, in the Chancery Division and we have relinquished the contested probate actions to them as *quid pro quo*. We are now called the Family Division and we have two very good female judges and I trust that we present a very avant garde profile to the general public.

When I was appointed, I was not yet a Bencher. It takes much longer to become a Bencher in some Inns of Court than in others. The Inner Temple takes the longest time, about seven or eight years after you take silk. There are only two other ways to be elected, one of which is by becoming an auditor, and the other by being selected as a worthy junior counsel who will represent the views of the junior Bar in the councils of the Inn, as he does not propose to take silk.

Neither of these is very satisfactory. Most of the juniors change their minds and take silk and most of the rest die or take a job. The auditors don't do much auditing, and have a senior bencher as permanent auditor over them, at the moment Sir Ashton Roskill, until recently the chairman of the Monopolies Commission, a very busy man indeed, and they have also the assistance of a professional chartered accountant if they want it. Their appointment is generally the result of some harmless nepotism : indeed it is difficult to see how such an appointment could be achieved without a friend at Court. But what is overlooked too often is that every time an auditor is elected a potential future Master Treasurer is being elected, as the boy who is made auditor is likely to be many years younger than the silk who has been slogging along for seven or eight years. And election to Master Treasurer almost always goes by seniority.

I was elected a Bencher, after my three and a half years in silk, because judges are supernumerary to the establishment and don't have to fill a vacancy. All the same, I shall be about ninety-four before I come up for the position of Master Treasurer, and I rather think that, even if I am still here, I shall probably decline it.

Once appointed a judge, I could no longer sit in Hall at luncheon below the salt with my chums, and as there was a week or so to elapse before the procedure to elect me to the Bench had been complied with, I was reduced once again to eating fattening sandwiches in my room with a glass of water, the former provided by Bridget, the latter by HM Government. It was like 1946 all over again.

For nine years before the war I had sat at the same table. After the war, first in the Niblett Hall, and then in the new Hall built to take the place of that destroyed by Hitler, I sat with my friends drinking barley water (twopence) at the same table. It was rather as though one had a season ticket for the seat. When I first came to the Bar a number of veterans still sat down to luncheon in their top hats, and at the buffet at the end of the Hall it was not done to stand and eat unless your head was covered. There was also a tremendous amount of raising of hats to the judiciary who would gravely respond. Very few people wear hats nowadays unless they are over sixty, and one of my younger brethren has told me that the only reason that he wears a hat is to take it off to the few who take theirs off to him.

But one feature has remained constant since I was called in 1930, and that and the Long Vacation may have something to do with the longevity of judges.

This feature is that it is almost unheard of for anyone in the body of the Hall to take alcohol with his meal. Before the war there was a man in a top hat who used to have a whisky, and heads were shaken about him. Although an advocate of some distinction he never became a Bencher and eventually retired to a County Court Judgeship. One man at our table sometimes had a quarter of a bottle of Beaujolais but that was considered very daring and no one followed his example. He wasn't a London practitioner and this may have been to celebrate the fact that he had got the day off.

When you became a Bencher, you ordered a bottle of sherry for the chums you had left behind, and drank their health from the High Table, and that was the extent of a lifetime's alcoholic excess at luncheon in the Inner Temple.

To be elected a Bencher of one of the Inns of Court is a very great thing. It is a luncheon club with various grand evening activities, and above all with the duty of preserving usefully, for the nation as well as for the Bar, a very important part of our national heritage, if that phrase has not become debased through constant overuse.

The late Sir Malcolm Hilbery was wont to tell the apochryphal anecdote of the earnest student who was not very fluent in English and who answered the question : 'What do you know about debentures?' 'Dey are de ruling body of de Inn.' And they are. Now that the Senate of the Four Inns of Court and of the Bar has been set up, and the recommendations of the Pearce Committee on higher education adopted, it may be that their importance may be to some extent eroded. But it is still necessary to belong to one of the four Inns if you are to be called to the Bar and you will be very insensitive not to feel the atmosphere even of the Inner Temple Hall rebuilt, and not very well rebuilt, after Hitler's ravages.

Every student knows or should know where, as Shakespeare tells us, the Wars of the Roses started. Dull would the student be of soul who had not visited the Temple Church and seen the effigies of the Crusaders or looked at the Master's House from the site of which the then Master went by boat to Runnymede to try to reconcile King John with his barons. The late Lord Silsoe, our Treasurer some years ago, dealt in his *The Peculiarities of the Temple* with many fascinating matters of history of which too many of us know too little.

Lord Silsoe, then Malcolm Trustram-Eve, was the first Christian Governor of Bethlehem since the fall of Constantinople. He was appointed to that temporary post by Lord Allenby who entered Jerusalem humbly on foot, the cavalcade being led by my late cousin, Cyril, then Colonel, Farden. He was later killed in an Underground accident at the Temple Station, which was a non-event, while Norman Birkett who was travelling in the rear compartment, was unharmed. That was newsworthy.

The Temple Church is the property of the two Honourable Societies, the consecrated ground belonging to us, and the other side of Middle Temple Lane to the Middle Temple in whose Hall *Twelfth Night* is said to have received its first performance. The Temple Church is a Royal Peculiar, and when on 21st December 1966 the Queen and Prince Philip came to dine with Lord Silsoe and his fellow Benchers, the Archbishop took his place as a junior honorary member of the Bench rather than as the Primate. Terence Cuneo painted the occasion and I couldn't be there, as I thought it right to celebrate Papa's ninetieth birthday with a family party at June Farm.

The Sovereign is the Visitor of both Inns, and the Queen Mother and the Duke of Edinburgh are Royal Benchers of the Middle and of the Inner.

The peculiarities of the Temple come from the Bull of Pope Alexander

III of 1163. It was around that date that the Knights Templar moved down to the Temple from Holborn.

The freehold was vested in the Benchers of the two Inns by Royal Charter granted in August 1608 by King James I whom the school-children know as 'the wisest fool in Christendom'. He made no mistake that time.

From 1964 to 1966 I had hilarious holidays with my brother Peter and his wife Pamela and their two boys at their villa in the Algarve – at the warm Spanish end near Monte Gordo and Villa Real di San Antonio – both at Whitsun and in the Summer. They also invited Judith and a girl friend of hers one year. I used to bore everyone absolutely stiff with anecdotes of Grandpa and in the evenings, to the light of the oil lamps, we got down to a serious session of 'Woodland Happy Families'. It was very pleasant, and I could rise early in the morning and walk for about an hour down to Monte Gordo in bare feet on the sand, and then back again to Altura without meeting a soul.

Whether you could swim at Whitsun depended on whether the festival was early or late. In those days we had not become entirely secular, and actually considered that Whitsun Bank Holiday had some-thing to do with Whit Sunday. But it was always the most tremendous fun even when the Portuguese men-of-war manifested themselves on the beach.

One year the house was over full and I volunteered to sleep on a camp bed in the car port. It was beautifully cool but, night after night, I was visited by stray dogs who seemed to have a great affection for me. This I found tiresome and the house was often awakened by petulant cries of 'Go away, go away'. But for the presence of children my language might have become stronger, but dogs are not polyglots and it couldn't have mattered. I remember the late Colonel Birley in 1941 saying in inspiring tones, 'The Royal Gloucestershire Hussars will advance – *iggori, imshi, rho,*' (My Arabic is not very good), without having the slightest effect upon the dogs of Sidi Bish.

CHAPTER SEVENTEEN

Family Multiplication

In 1965 came the great occasion of my life. I was at Birmingham with
Owlie and Harry Phillimore, they doing the crime while I did the
civil work and divorce matters. This new allocation of work was a
splendid decision made by Viscount Dilhorne (ex-Reggie Manningham-
Buller) when Lord Chancellor and prevents the Divorce Judges from
getting stale trying nothing but divorce. Nowadays there is so much
crime that the Queen's Bench Judges try nothing else for two thirds
of the year and are at risk of being sent to the Old Bailey during the
one third that they are in London. It must be a soul destroying life for
them and, if anyone makes so bold as to criticise the length of the Long
Vacation, I always reply that a Queen's Bench Judge gives up a lucrative practice, which he probably operates from home, in exchange for
spending most of the year away from home for fifteen solid years before
he becomes entitled to a pension, simply because he thinks that longer
holidays compensate for lesser earnings. The lucky Chancery Judges
are in London all the year round as usually is the Admiralty Judge. It
may be remembered that I wanted the PDA Division largely because it
involved only fourteen weeks away from home, but, since my appointment, that term of the contract has been unilaterally changed in that we
now go out for twenty weeks, which in fact I didn't object to as all
the children are now grown up, and married.

At Birmingham, Owlie had a marshal who was a Crown counsel in
Hong Kong, one Hopkinson, who very kindly got us silk pyjamas from
that colony, and who wanted his daughter to be educated at Benenden,
where Judith was at the time, and which had become rather more
difficult to get into once Princess Anne had been sent there. Harry
Phillimore had a marshal called Kirkwood, who had two half-sisters,
and had had two whole sisters, at Benenden, and while Harry and I
were playing billiards with the marshals the subject of the school cropped
up occasionally. We played a lot of billiards most enjoyably because
Owlie used to go to his room at half past nine, having dominated the

dinner table and entertained us all for two hours, the marshals open mouthed and more or less speechless after they had said grace, while his brother judges acted as feeds. He was very entertaining about the first war and about Bertrand Russell for whom he had appeared in a divorce, apart from so many other matters. The marshals used to take it in turns to walk round the golf course with me before breakfast. It is a time of day when I am rather less voluble than usual but I can remember, with amusement now, having to undergo a lengthy cross-examination about the styles of Hastings and Birkett, also in cross-examination. It did not amuse me then.

[Owlie said to me a few days before I wrote this : 'You know, Neville, you always say that you wouldn't do something "for all the tea in China".' I said, 'Yes.' He said : 'I'm re-reading the Waverley Novels, and I've found it in *Rob Roy*. I've turned the page down for you.' I thought that pretty good for an old man of eighty-nine.]

I had never taken a marshal, and it was not until the next year, 1966 that I began to take Esmond during the early part of his Long Vacation from Cambridge when the house at home stood empty, Papa having gone to stay elsewhere while I was on circuit. The boys were very good in the summer holidays, Nigel fire-fighting in the Rockies, and Esmond helping to lay a road in Indianapolis, and thanks to Miriam Odgers and Peter and Pam and many others we managed to provide entertainment for Judith.

I have a feeling that this vital Assize of 1965 was in November and December and that towards the end Norman Richards QC came as a commissioner (always known as 'the Commissionaire') to help with the crime. If so, it must be the Assize when he and I had a game of croquet on 18th December, after I had fallen into a bunker in the dark on our morning walk. He, bless him, became Sir Norman Richards.

Harry's marshal was a very tactful young man and laughed at my jokes. I warmed to him. That he was a very astute young man and one who was destined to do me the greatest kindness, I didn't know. One day he nobbled me and said in an innocent manner :

'Judge, do you do any public work?'

Guiltily, I confessed that I didn't.

He said, 'Would you consider being Chairman of the Benenden Parents' Association?'

I said, 'I shouldn't think so,' and he looked a little crestfallen.

So I thought to console him. 'Oh ! I dare say I might, but I am sure that they wouldn't ask me.'

'Oh! yes they would.'

'How do you know?'

'My mother is the secretary.'

'Well, let's wait and see, shall we?'

And so the matter was left. In the fullness of time, I received a visit from Sir Ronald Harris, a very high-powered individual, four years younger than I was, but who had been in the Cabinet Secretariat during the war and was soon to take over as first Church Estates Commissioner from Lord Silsoe. He is now the Chairman of the Benenden School Council. I was all alone, the women having gone home as it was Saturday afternoon, and Papa was oblivious to everything as he sat in the granary at the other end of the house, which we had turned into a television room for him, watching the semi-finals of the English ladies back-stroke swimming competition or something equally fascinating, with the volume turned up very high.

It was very good of Harris to come over from Stoke D'Abernon, and I wished that I had had a housekeeper or someone to give him tea. He didn't stay very long however and, although he asked if I would be interested in the job, he left me rather unnerved by not going so far as to offer it to me. I felt that perhaps I had failed my viva. But I did receive the offer later and accepted it, having ascertained from my guest that it was not a very onerous appointment. When Judith eventually left school I had to leave the Benenden Council and resign as Chairman of the Parents' Association, being no longer a parent. Betty Clarke, the headmistress, and I decided that the chap to ask to succeed me would be General Sir Harold Redman who had been Governor of Gibraltar. Again I was a little worried for he had commanded a brigade in the desert when I had been a little major. But I asked him to luncheon in the Temple and introduced him to a few Law Lords and all went merry as a marriage bell, and he kindly took on the post. When I took on the chairmanship, I had to make a visit to Millbank to be present when Harris resigned and handed over to Faulks. A parting speech of thanks was made by Mary Dilhorne, wife to the ex-Lord Chancellor, and I met 'the secretary' for the first time.

She was very helpful and sent me some files of the previous proceedings for me to peruse. Some correspondence had been enclosed in error, from which I was interested to learn that Lord Bradford had refused the chairmanship, and that they were at their wits' end to find someone to take it on.

The next time that we met was at what I always call 'the annual outing' at Benenden although it is more seriously called 'Hobbies Day'. She decided that I was very arrogant and I thought her somewhat offensive. After such a splendid start our courtship moved on unchecked. I did have the good sense to take advice before trying to set off on matrimony again. I went to my friend Bazil Wingate-Saul, a very learned County Court Judge, lawn tennis with whom every Saturday had solaced my years of widowerhood. (Years later he became very disturbed as he feared that he might have misinformed my 'healer' as to the date of the death of Mahomet.)

'Is she of suitable age ?'

'Yes.'

'Does she irritate you ?'

'Good God, no.'

'Then I should go ahead.'

Short and to the point and just what I wanted to hear.

Bazil, 'the wit of the Northern Circuit,' died, to the grief of many, in October 1975. I was extremely upset and fear that I did not do him justice in the obituary notice which I wrote and which *The Times* was good enough to print. I won't repeat it here as I have a little to say about him later on.

Judith and I went to Wittenham House for the new year of 1966-67 and it was not long after that that I became engaged to be married to Elizabeth for I have always been impulsive, and it was as well. Andrew, Harry Phillimore's ex-marshal, installed me in what he called 'the judicial wing' where I was very comfortable and we had a very happy New Year. No one had let on about Elizabeth's previous matrimonial career. If they had, I doubt if I would have thought myself worthy to propose.

Her father was killed in the first war, and she never knew him. I have only met one man who did, the late senior partner of Dawson and Co, the family solicitors, who had been up with him at Magdalen College, Oxford. She lived with her mother and aunt in Reading where she was born. She went to Benenden where her four daughters followed her in due course. She became 'unofficially engaged', as it was termed in those golden and unsophisticated days, to Tristram Kirkwood, while she was still at school, captain of the school, which really meant Captain of Games, for she was a great lacrosse player (an exercise which I have never seen performed). She was chosen for an England trial, but it was foggy, and she rather naughtily spent the afternoon with Tristram. She never played for England.

Tristram was killed in action in Holland in 1944 and left her with three children of whom the youngest, my friend the marshal, had the Bishop of Reading for his godfather. Elizabeth had always hoped that the Bishop would marry her mother, for he was a great family friend, but her mother died before Andrew, the marshal, was born.

She was in her twenties and with three young children and she carried on. Then one day the Bishop asked if he might marry her. He was of course many years older than she was, but he was a most remarkable man. He and Owlie are the only people of whom I have heard who have ridden with every pack of hounds in the country, and he was accustomed to ride round his diocese. She said, 'Yes'. Two more children. Two more pupils for Benenden. Age takes its toll, and he died at about the same time as Bridget. Overworked widow, sad and bored widower. We were made for each other.

The reason why I would have hesitated to propose and try to live up to the standard of her previous husbands is shown in their citations in *The Times* which I set out without any further comment, except that you must remember that I am rather an emotional character. Tristram was born after me and Arthur a number of years before, but I put Tristram first, because he was husband number one. And if you don't understand why I am proud to be number three, I shall be very surprised.

Tristram was killed on 17th November 1944, a week after his birthday, and the following appeared in *The Times*:

Personal tribute – Major T. G. H. Kirkwood. A correspondent writes:

'Major Tristram Kirkwood RE whose death in action is reported, joined the directing staff of the Sandhurst wing of the Staff College in July, 1943. The Sandhurst wing had been instituted to train staff officers of rather older vintage than those who normally graduate from Camberley; and it might well have been considered an ordeal for an officer still in his twenties to guide, to instruct, and to assess men who were for the most part considerably older than himself and of extensive and varied civilian backgrounds. If it was an ordeal for Kirkwood – and he gave no sign that it was – it was one that he triumphantly survived.

'It was a great disappointment to find myself in the syndicate of so young an instructor,' one of the officers confided to me at the end of our first course, 'but after being in his syndicate for a day or two I realised how lucky I was to be with a man so well versed in his profession and having so clear a mind and such a flair for exposition.'

It was a spontaneous tribute in which all his students would have joined – Kirkwood was that comparatively rare product, an officer equally equipped by nature for success on the staff or as a regimental officer. He went to the Staff College with experience as diverse as command of a West African field company, and a chair in the Directorate of Military Training at the War Office. On leaving the Staff College he returned, to his great satisfaction, to regimental duty in command of a field company in 21 Army Group. His great abilities, vital energy, – at the Sandhurst Wing he was universally known as Dynamite – and real interest in men made him a born commander. As such he was happy, and as such he was killed. An officer of his quality must have been destined for great things in the Army. If he had not chosen the Army, his abilities, his judgment, his confidence, and his singular maturity might have made him an administrator of the first rank.

Kirkwood put me in mind of Santayana's tribute, 'The Englishman carries his English weather in his heart wherever he goes; it becomes a cool spot in the desert, and a steady and sane oracle among all the deliriums of mankind'.

It is a tragedy that his great abilities and staunch personality have not been suffered to endure into the post-war world, where they could have helped so much.

Who the 'correspondent' was, I have no idea. I think that he must be in his late seventies by now, but I should like to meet him if he is still alive.

From that to something a generation before. Arthur was put in for the Victoria Cross but did not get it. *The Times* newspaper records amongst those who had been awarded the Military Cross:

'Rev A. G. Parham, Temporary Chaplain 4th Class (Precentor of Christ Church, Oxford).'

It only condescends to detail with the citation of one of those who had received an award, Arthur Parham.

Mr A. G. Parham won his Military Cross for gallantry in Gallipoli. His brigade was in the attack on the Turkish position at Suvla on August 21st when the shrubs on the Anafarta plain caught fire. With the help of his servant he rescued many wounded men and carried them to a place of safety beyond reach of the flames, and the following day, obtaining a large number of volunteers from his own brigade to act as stretcher bearers, he was chiefly instrumental in evacuating the wounded from Chocolate Hill. After the battle he remained with the brigade in the trenches for ten weeks under constant fire, ministering to the wounded and burying the dead. He regularly celebrated the Holy Communion early each morning, some days at two or more positions in the trenches, and during the period mentioned administered the Blessed Sacrament to over one thousand communicants. Subsequently he accompanied the brigade in the campaign against the Senussi on the western frontier of Egypt.

I suppose that it is because I am getting old, but I cannot read that citation without tears.

*

I had three unmarried children, and she had five, only one of whom was married, and one of the things we had to decide was where we were to live.

The married daughter was Juliet who had already produced three children and was soon to provide a fourth. Two boys, two girls, in that order – very satisfactory. She is married to Michael Sutton-Scott-Tucker who farms a large acreage near Dartmouth and they live in the most beautiful farmhouse. His real name is Sutton, and he is the son of Air Marshal Sir Bertine Sutton who died a long time ago. His mother I have never met. She is a Wedderburn, the head of the family being Lord Dundee, Hereditary Royal Standard Bearer for Scotland. Michael is rightly proud of his ancestry. The Scott-Tucker bit is because his aunt married a Scott-Tucker who was the Lord of the Manor and kept his own pack of hounds, and when the old gentleman died he left it to Michael provided that he assumed the name of 'Scott-Tucker' otherwise the whole shooting match would go to University College, Oxford, which, with Professor Goodhart in residence, was not without means. So it was worth while assuming the name, even if the boys do get teased at school sometimes, and a lot of land had to be sold for death duties. Farming is his idea of bliss and he is a working farmer working very long hours, and he knows about, and has a lot of, wine. A very pleasant life for a young couple and when you consider that Juliet is tremendously efficient as well as looking a very attractive twenty-two year old (although she is thirty-seven) he has little of which to complain, unless he is destroyed by the contemplated Wealth Tax, or cannot sell his cattle.

We now, thank God, have been allowed to buy their estate carpenter's cottage, have spent much more money on it than we can afford, have put in a heated swimming pool and a croquet lawn, have a rural view (for we are in the valley behind Stoke Fleming) the like of which cannot in my opinion be equalled, are fifteen minutes' drive from Dartmouth with its different type of extreme beauty, are five minutes' drive from Blackpool Sands which are beautiful in another kind of way, and are the two luckiest old buzzards alive.

Juliet being settled, we were still left with seven, and neither Wittenham House opposite the famous Clumps and hard by the Thames in the tiny village of Little Wittenham, nor June Farm, were quite big enough. What we should have done was to have sold both houses, and gone into a fresh home where we all should have started at scratch. But I was selfishly determined to take my bride and her brood to June Farm, for I loved it so much. Elizabeth never made a murmur of protest, and I won, without realising what a pig I was.

We spent most of the Long Vacation of 1967 at Wittenham House sorting out the accumulations of two husbands and two families over many years. Papa came to stay, which was very sweet of Elizabeth who was recovering from a major operation which she underwent almost immediately after we were married. She has had five altogether in under ten years, and it is marvellous now that she has got two new hips that really work, and is in better health than I am, which, as she is about ten years younger, is as it should be. Papa enjoyed himself immensely, poking his nose into everything, more out of an old man's inquisitiveness than to any malice on his part.

We had been married, as I have already said, from the Birmingham lodgings. It was as romantic as it could be, considering our mature age. She arrived in time for luncheon on Friday in her Volvo and a new hat, was greeted warmly by Mr and Mrs Green, the butler and housekeeper, and introduced to my brother judges who were naturally very charming. We had an excellent meal, and went off to Lincoln in my Mercedes, as I wanted to drive. We stayed the night with Kenneth and Katherine Riches and Kenneth, the Bishop of Lincoln, married us in the Cathedral in the morning. After luncheon with the Riches we motored back to Birmingham for our 'honeymoon'. There had been present at the ceremony two Riches, two Faulks, the Diocesan Registrar and the Verger, not like her last wedding at Christ Church Cathedral, Oxford, or mine at St James the Less, Lower Barnet, but right and proper for all that. As most of our two families could not manage to get to Lincoln, we thought it better to have none of them. The reason that we went to Lincoln was because once upon a time Arthur and Kenneth, then Bishop of Dorchester, had both been Suffragans of the Bishop of Oxford.

I was a bit nervous for her when we got back to face one judge who was a widower, and one judge who had not his wife there. And there is a great deal of protocol in Lodgings which can be baffling if you don't take care. The Senior Judge was the representative of the Queen and in that capacity always went in first to dinner, the junior judge said grace if there was no marshal present, and the Senior Judge sat with his back to the fire or to where the fire would have been, if there had been one, which there wasn't. When the judges leave the lodgings in the morning, however, the procession is inverted and the order is Under Sheriffs, High Sheriff, junior judge, second judge, Senior Judge, (and one Senior Judge used to have his wife curtseying in the hall as the great man, temporarily royal, passed by), followed by the marshals in their top hats and tail coats.

Arrived at the official cars, way is made for the Senior Judge and a great deal of bowing by everybody else takes place while he enters first. At the Castle or Town Hall or whatever it may be, it is important to remember to let the Senior Judge alight first and to stand still if there are trumpeters, or you may disappear from sight while they are still hard at it, which they don't like. Occasionally as on Owlie's eightieth birthday, police horses are laid on for the birthday boy to inspect, or, as on Jimmy Cassels' eightieth birthday, the band alarmingly strikes up 'He's a fine old English gentleman'. For future judges: 'When in doubt, stand still and bow'. It looks good and gives you time to see what's cooking, when you may proceed. And hold your shoulders back, particularly if you are in commission (which means trying the crime) and are wearing a full-bottomed wig. I should also add for the good of your morale, in case you don't know it already, in precedence you rank above a bold bad baronet, but you are still below an Earl's younger son who, somewhat surprisingly, precedes the Chancellor of the Exchequer, the Lord Chief Justice of England, the Master of the Rolls, and the Lords Justices of Appeal as well as you. My own view, although the Garter King of Arms may not agree with me, is that when I retired I ceased to be the Honourable Sir Neville Faulks, ceased to rank above a baronet, and become just another old Knight Bachelor.

Women, on the whole, are expected to be seen and not heard, not that that really mattered with Owlie about, when no one could have got a word in edgeways, regardless of sex.

I need not have been nervous: thirteen years as a bishop's wife, and Divisional Commissioner of Girl Guides had obviously taught her to say the right thing at the right time and, if it was shop, ten years as a Justice of the Peace was long enough to avoid her putting her foot in it too deeply.

So although a honeymoon in lodgings, as 'guests of the judges' who haven't asked you, sounds unpromising enough, it was very enjoyable indeed, even though I was away in court for the better part of the day.

Poor Elizabeth had a pretty rotten time that summer of 1967. A houseful of children, and Papa smoking his pipe all over the place, and, while she had to rest every afternoon, blest if I didn't get myself laid up for a fortnight with gout. Cheap dry Cyprus sherry I indict as the offender, but I have no doubt that any skilful advocate could ensure its acquittal.

Eventually I recovered and went on with the job of collecting many sacks of ancient and unwanted correspondence, greatly assisted by Kent, the gardener and general factotum, who had driven Elizabeth to her first wedding. At last the great day came for our final move to June Farm. We had been to-ing and fro-ing with bits and pieces for a very long time until I knew that rather dreary road through Wallingford, Henley, Wargrave, Twyford, Bracknell, Bagshot *et alia* so much by heart that I would dream it at night.

Papa was now rising ninety-one and had gone on to a stronger brew of tobacco, if that were possible, for Saint Bruno Rough Cut was enough to make me feel unwell, and he used to smoke it in the car when Elizabeth was there, because he sensed that she was so newly married that she wouldn't object. Thus he used to get away with it, although the stench was unbelievable. He was also feeling rather powerful because before I could get the Archbishop's licence to marry in a Cathedral, I had had to get his written consent to the marriage. I was fifty-nine at the time, and it is a very remarkable law. He didn't give it at once.

'Are you going to throw me out?' he asked (this is what I always used to call the *King Lear* complex).

'Of course not.'

'Oh, very well then. I'll sign.'

'Thank you very much, Daddy.'

That was a word from my youth which I had not used for many

years for by this time I usually called Papa 'Grandpa' like the children, or even 'Pa' which is what Elizabeth's children call me.

We sold Wittenham House to the local doctor who put in a reasonable bid before we had got it on to the market. One cottage went to Peggy who had helped in the laundry for a long time and of whom Elizabeth was very fond, for a price that was not inflated. One cottage is still inhabited by a splendid old-age pensioner who pays very little indeed, and one we kept for emergencies after very nearly selling it. Jenny, our doctor daughter, has now bought it, and enjoys it very much.

So the problem was to house the two of us, Papa, who had to have a whacking great double bedroom to himself as he had been there for thirteen years, three children of mine and four of hers, with a spare room or two for visitors.

We managed. That is, she managed. We built a new tennis court and improved the swimming-pool. The croquet lawn with its dips down to the side, known as the 'Cresta Run' where you had to play out of a bog, was left untouched. She gutted and entirely reorganised the kitchen quarters. The improvement was fantastic, but it was not inexpensive. The architect disappeared at an early date, and Elizabeth and the builder worked together. The result was so successful that we more or less lived in the kitchen and the dining room was only used on state occasions so much so that I was constrained to refer to it sometimes as the 'parlour', an expression which nobody under sixty understands.

But the real conundrum was the housing of the brood. I think that it was my idea to convert the barn at the south of the walled garden at the front of the house into three bedrooms, a bathroom and a lavatory. I had found it as a gigantic wood shed when I bought the place in 1954, and had turned it into a ping-pong room with Globe Vernicke bookcases filled with Triang toys belonging to the children, and a large radio-gramophone and other articles of equipment belonging to Richard. I also had an ancient upright piano in there on which Papa aged ninety and Uncle Sydney aged eighty-six played a duet the score of which I have recently mislaid.

Although it may have been my idea initially, the whole project was carried out by Elizabeth with Mr Fletcher, the builder. Mark you, I couldn't do very much about it because I was commuting to and fro every day to the Law Courts when I was not on Circuit.

The work went on, frustrated by the necessity of Town Planning Permission, of visits from the Fine Arts Commission and Uncle Tom

Cobbleigh and all. I used to point out that, whereas the granary was a scheduled building which I must not touch without many kinds of permission, the particular barn, which seemed to have been built in about 1850 was a different architectural cup of tea. In vain; but at last permission came through. I was in a hopeless position, for one of Her Majesty's Judges can scarcely have a glass of sherry, let alone breach the Building Regulations.

We took Kent the gardener and his wife to Reigate Heath with us, for Elizabeth had known them all her life. We bought a cottage so near that their garden ran into ours and it ought always to have been part of the same property. That wasn't cheap, for the owner, who had used it for his own staff, very sensibly realised that I felt that I must have it. Kent and Win were being uprooted after many years, and poor Kenty was going to be the second gardener. But it wasn't too bad for them, for when at last we moved to London we got them a bungalow near their married daughter at Poole, and they seem to be very happy.

By October 1967 the whole lot were housed, and her children were housed without complaint – more perhaps because they were well brought up than because they enjoyed moving from the house they had known and loved for so long. I must be very insensitive for I really believed that this exceedingly expensive operation had been a triumph. And so it might have been if time had stood still. But it has a tiresome habit of not doing so.

The first to go was Nigel who was bored with the Bar and went off to Teheran to a post with the Persian Oil Consortium. There he won the Iranian Squash Racquets Championship several times, met and married a delightful wife, had two very attractive children, and is now living in Cornwall and is a solicitor, and has a third son. Poor Caroline : she so wants a daughter, but children are so expensive nowadays. That left a really superb bedroom vacant.

Then the 'marshal' got married. Delightful wife once more, but another bedroom vacant. They were married in the Temple Church with my two old friends, Kenneth Riches and Bobbie Milburn, officiating, which was very pleasing.

Then came a stream of weddings from June Farm, two of which emptied a bedroom. First, Annie, the Bishop's elder daughter, married a submariner, Johnny, presently commanding a submarine, as a Lieutenant-Commander. Second, Richard, Bridget's half brother, who married Isobel, of whom we are both very fond. Third, Philippa, who married Anthony, PSC (which means to the uninitiated, that he has passed through the Staff College, like Tristram), who is now in command of a battery in Germany.

Judith went to Australia and Hong Kong and Jennifer seemed to spend a great deal of time at Cape Cod, Massachusetts. She had gone back to Oxford again, happily with good results. She is now a registered medical practitioner, highly qualified, and madly attractive. Judith's husband who was at Gordonstoun and Balliol, speaks Thai, French, German, Cantonese, and Mandarin, plays the flute, and is a great salmon fisherman. Lucky girl!

It all seems too good to be true and no doubt I shall be brought to a sense of reality before long. Meanwhile, Esmond has gone to the Newcastle Bar and become happily married.

And do they breed?

Nigel	3
Juliet	4
Jennifer	Not yet.
Andrew	3
Esmond	2
Annie	3
Philippa	2
Judith	One of these days. Married on 22nd February 1975 and living in Brussels)
Richard	2
	19 to date.

Elizabeth has a very complicated 'granny's bracelet', with different insignia for each family and the name and the birthday of the child on the back. It saves a great deal of ferreting about in diaries to find out who has to have the next present. She made one error but even that may help. She has two grandchildren called 'Sophia'. One she has spelt correctly, but in the other her remote Bulgarian ancestry had let her down and it reads 'Sofia'.

In 1948 when morals were still almost Victorian, my darling Elizabeth, thirty-one and newly a Bishop's wife, went down to Reading on a Monday morning. To her horror, several windows of the largest store were filled with naked models. With her handbag at the ready, she stormed in to complain. Apologies and protestations and all the models were covered with sheets forthwith. This could scarcely have happened today. I so much admire Mrs Whitehouse.

I first had trouble in my left hand in 1954 when I thought that the nasty marks on my palm and the pain that went with it was something to do with my tennis racquet. I am left-handed. As the years went on, it became much worse and the psoriasis spread over my whole body leaving me in permanent discomfort, best described by Mr Cecil King as 'living in a hair shirt'.

I started accordingly to walk about in Court, for to sit still for a long time was agony. You can't scratch in public and the only alternative is to walk about and get a little air on the body. This was not understood, and I became the eccentric judge.

Humorous hits at the annual dinner of the PD & A Division:— 'Our peripatetic judge' and 'a day in Mr Justice Faulks' court is a day in the life of Groucho Marx'. Quite fair: and if I had said that I didn't do it because I liked it, but because I had to, it would have spoiled the joke, so I said nothing.

Years ago there was a High Court Divorce Judge who was also experienced in Admiralty matters. It was before the last war and his name was Mr Justice Langton. He was the president for the time of the All-England Lawn Tennis and Croquet Club at Wimbledon. He too was restless. Lord Pearce has given his permission for me to tell this anecdote which was first recounted to me by Harry Phillimore. George Langton used to walk up and down the bench just as I do, and on one occasion in 1937 or thereabouts he turned to Mr Holroyd Pearce, then a young and possibly frightened man appearing for the Queen's Proctor:

'Tell me, Mr Pearce', as he turned the corner, 'is there no legal Latin maxim to help me on which way I ought to go when the evidence is so doubtful and conflicting?'

'Perhaps, my Lord, *solvitur ambulando.*'

I have never had a chance to say anything like that but I wish that I had. As a matter of fact I did once say something very witty to Judge Clements in the Ashford County Court but, unfortunately, I cannot remember what it was.

CHAPTER EIGHTEEN

A Winner and a Loser

As I have already said, in the autumn of 1973, it seemed as though I had got gout as well as psoriasis. I felt very unwell at the beginning of 1974 and eventually the wizards diagnosed it as arthritis supervening the psoriasis. I had lost much of the use of both hands and couldn't write for more than a minute or two at a time, although I was as fit as a fiddle apart from that.

I went into hospital which was absolute hell. I hadn't experienced anything like it since I brought German Measles back to Uppingham in 1923. They had not yet started to say that we were Fascist pigs because we were not on the National Health : but the nurses were very bored, and the room was like a cell. Then I was told that I couldn't take the two treatments prescribed for me. Elizabeth was delighted, and off we went to a wonderful 'healer' who does not charge for her services and does not desire publicity. I had been told that the arthritis in my hands was 'progressive', and that I should take cortisone orally, and injections of gold into my fingers. I didn't fancy that. I am stupidly scared of drugs. Certainly my GP seemed to think that I was silly but the fact is that after four months with my 'healer' my psoriasis receded somewhat and I hope but doubt that one day it will disappear altogether, while my 'progressive' arthritis has been halted.

I have had two crusades since I have been on the Bench. In both cases, you will not be surprised to hear that I am satisfied that I was right. One was a case about an immigrant Czechoslovak couple called Novotnik, in which they collected five Judges of the Court of Appeal, who unanimously decided that I had talked a lot of nonsense. Some years later I was gratified to read in the Law Reports, by accident, for they are not my bedside reading, – that Lord Denning had been gracious enough to eat his words and declare that Novotnik had been wrongly decided in the Court of Appeal. Good for Faulks' morale, but the unfortunate middle-European, who must have been substantially out of pocket as a result of the decision, would probably not have been amused. However I don't suppose he reads the Law Reports and no doubt, like me, he did not receive a copy of the later judgment.

It was all about an Act of Parliament which says that if some legally aided character sues you and you, who have to pay for yourself, win then, in certain circumstances you can get your costs out of the Law Society. I said he could : they said he could not.

The other one I lost. I said that an Act of Parliament meant what it said, and the Court of Appeal said that it meant something else. In another case on the same point a different Court of Appeal agreed with me but was not prepared to go so far as to say that the earlier court had decided as it had *per incuriam* – which is, as I have previously indicated, a polite way of saying that they were temporarily certifiable.

And the Law of England seems to be that if you want to get rid of your wife, give her a lot of gin, tuck her up in bed with the lodger, and present a petition the next day saying that she has committed adultery and you find it intolerable to live with her because she often wears pink pyjamas or, if you like, for no reason at all. I am unaware of the reaction of the Vatican to this interesting piece of jurisprudence.

It is only right to say that my brother Mr Justice Lloyd-Jones took a different view from me on this particular point, and the dons thought it all very exciting. How many angels could dance on the point of a pin wasn't in it, and all the little boys were lectured about it, the experts disagreeing with me for the most part.

My brother Peter's boy, Edward, was one of these fortunate pupils. He wrote the unpopular opinion and his tutor said, 'I see that you agree with Mr Justice Faulks, Forks.' The boy kept a straight face.

The matter in dispute was this. In old days if your spouse committed adultery you could be granted a divorce, unless you had connived at it, that is, had organised it or approved it, or unless you had condoned it, that is, had forgiven it. Then, in 1969, Parliament enacted a new statue which abolished the concepts of connivance and condonation, and decreed that 'the sole ground on which a petition for divorce may be presented to the Court by either party to a marriage shall be that the marriage has broken down irretrievably'.

However, Parliament didn't leave it there, but went on to provide that, although the marriage may have broken down irretrievably, the Judge wasn't allowed to say so, except in certain circumstances.

The Court hearing a petition for divorce shall not hold the marriage to have broken down irretrievably unless the petitioner satisfies the Court of one or more of the following facts, that is to say,

(a)   that the respondent has committed adultery and the petitioner finds it intolerable to live with the respondent

So two things have to be proved instead of one. Then our legislators continued in S.3(3):

Where the parties to the marriage have lived with each other for any period or periods, after it became known to the petitioner that the respondent had, since the celebration of the marriage, committed adultery, then,

(b)   if the length of that period or of those periods together exceeded six months, the petitioner shall not be entitled to rely on that adultery for the purposes of the said section (1) (a)

That amounts to saying that if you have tolerated the adultery for six months you can't be heard to say that it is intolerable.

So I didn't have much hesitation in saying: 'I think that common-sense tells you that where the finding that has to be made is that the respondent has committed adultery and the petitioner finds it intolerable to live with the respondent it means *'and in consequence* of the adultery the petitioner finds it intolerable to live with the respondent'.

Vincent Lloyd-Jones, founding himself on something that was submitted in a text-book, had earlier decided that the two phrases were independent of one another, so that you prove your wife's adultery, even though you have connived at it or condoned it, and truthfully state that her bad breath makes life intolerable, and your decree is there.

That seemed to me to be contrary to the sense of Section 3(3) quoted above, and I refused to follow him. The next thing that I heard was that the two conflicting decisions had been considered by a distinguished Court of Appeal two of the three members of which had in the past been Judges of the Divorce Division.

They knew that there were conflicting decisions on the point, but

Wallis's Cottage

Geriatric Occupational
Therapy 1977

Just over half the famil
Elizabeth's Sixtieth
Birthday

they did not ask for the help of the Queen's Proctor, they only heard the argument for one side as the wife was not represented; they made no reference to S3(3) in any of their judgments; they decided the point off the cuff without reserving judgment; and they decided, unkindest cut of all, that I was wrong.

I was astounded, as were, I believe, all my brethren with the exception of the President, Sir George Baker. I was not favoured with a copy of the judgment, as it was not an appeal from me, and it was not until the case appeared in the Law Reports in the following year that I realised that, apparently, no reference had been made to S3(3) at all.

Meanwhile, as I have said, another distinguished Court of Appeal, two members of which had in the past been Judges of the Divorce Division, had to consider the point. They didn't like the decision of the other Court but they were bound to follow it unless they were prepared to say that it was decided *per incuriam* which they were not prepared to do, being kindly people. But they went as near as they safely could.

One Lord Justice said:

Only one party was represented. It would have been perhaps happier, these different views having been expressed as to the construction of the Section, to have heard an argument from the Queen's Proctor on this matter. But, as I say, the Court heard only one side. The other matter with regard to that, is that the wording of S.3(3) is directly treating the adultery as being the fons et origo (the fount and origin) perhaps, of the intolerability. In view of the fact that this Statute is comparatively new and is frequently called into operation, it might be desirable that the matter should come in some form before the House of Lords, so that the profession may have clear guidance about it.

Another Lord Justice went further:

The Court came to its conclusion without the help of argument on more than one side and apparently without considering S.3(3) of the 1969 Act for the light it might throw on S.2(1)(a). S.3(3) seems to me to fit much better the construction put on S.2(1)(a) by Faulks J., and to invite reconsideration of S.2(1)(a) by the House of Lords in an appropriate case. But I cannot assume that judges so familiar with divorce reform overlooked S.3(3), so as to enable us to treat their decision as given 'per incuriam' and, again on a unilateral argument, to interpret the sub-section differently.

Why in the world anyone should ever wish to go to the House of Lords on this academic point, I cannot imagine. My only hope is that one day I shall read in my retirement that Lord Denning, who will surely go on as Master of The Rolls for ever (as he is said recently, at the age of seventy-nine, to have purchased a new robe), has again candidly admitted that his decision was wrong. He expressed an opinion in the Court of Appeal the other day with which Lord Justice Lawton agreed, although Lord Justice Bridge and, ultimately, an unanimous House of Lords did not.

'What,' said the Judge with whom the majority of the Court of Appeal had disagreed, 'made fearless Fred agree with Tom?'

'Surely', said Lord Justice Stamp, 'you know. He who would valiant be 'gainst all disaster, let him in constancy follow the Master.'

Bazil Wingate-Saul was a man of parts. He was a do-it-yourself man and could make things. I could never do that; and he was an all-round games player. In the old days, I used to beat him at lawn tennis but by the time I sold June Farm it was a very close thing, although he was older than I was.

Bazil wrote entertaining poetry and he was kind enough to say that I may quote some of it here. I would like to quote two. The first was written in 1961 when a mysterious figure made an ephemeral appearance in the foreign news pages of *The Times* newspaper, the 'Imam of Oman'.

The second I quote from 1969 after the Beeching report had caused a revolution in the Law. The metre is so good that it won't matter if the contents, like Gilbert's, are out of date a generation hence. I have only asked the author for permission to publish. I hope that Judge Peck won't take umbrage.

The Imam of Oman

Is his lineage lofty, noble and narrow?
Does his blood run blue to the very marrow?
Did he spend his formative years at Harrow?
Or is he a yeoman,
The Imam of Oman?

Is his pigment copper, coffee or puce?
Are his features flabby, his belly loose?
Does he waddle around in a white burnous
Like a snowman,
The Imam of Oman?

Is he a man of humble station?
Or does he with eastern ostentation
Live in a palace with sanitation,
A pull-and-let-go man,
The Imam of Oman?

Is his rebel army a rabble band
Vile with vermin and stained with sand?
Or is he, perhaps, on the other hand
A doughty foeman
The Imam of Oman?

Does he lead his men upon camel back
Over treeless desert and arid track,
Or bustle about in a Cadillac
Like a showman,
The Imam of Oman?

Without reward does he do as bid,
As a perfect gentleman lifts the lid?
Or is he, as others aver, a quid
Pro quo man,
The Imam of Oman?

When the toil and the heat of the day are done,
Does he squat on his hams in the setting sun
And furtively cram a raisin bun
Within his abdomen,
The Imam of Oman?

Or is he a slave to carnal lust?
Does he pass his leisure in parry and thrust,
Lashes to lashes and bust to bust
With a woman,
The Imam of Oman?

Verses recited at a dinner to celebrate
David Peck's appointment as a County Court Judge.

Men heard the wheels of Justice creak, laboriously turning,
'*Fiat Justitia*!', they cried, proud of their Latin learning.
The Bar, solicitors, the Press, for law reform were screeching;
The Chancellor was near despair – he sent for Dr Beeching.
Lord Beeching is a person whom no labyrinth non-plusses,
(He'd pulled up half the railway lines and filled the roads with buses)
A little problem such as this was well within his ambit,
He pondered it for several years – then played the Beeching gambit.
'The country's cluttered up,' he said, 'with courts of different sizes,
'With county courts and sessions courts, Old Baileys and assizes,
'With pompous men in varied garb, who multiply disorders,
'Like judges of the county courts, and chairmen and recorders.
'Come, dump upon the rubbish heap these antiquated drudges,
'Create a caste of supermen and call them Circuit Judges.
'Men such as England knew of yore, like Birkenhead and Carson,
'Who know the subtle difference 'twixt bottomry and arson,
'Whom mortgages do not dismay nor charging orders frighten,
'Who'll switch from sex at Sevenoaks to barratry at Brighton.'
The Chancellor was spell-bound when he read his Lordship's strictures.
'I'll build the galleries', he said, 'but who will find the pictures?
'What use are new Academies without the modern Platos?
'For who can offer fish and chips, unless he has potatoes?
'Still, oaks from little acorns grow and haste is overrated,
'Why, God took half a dozen days to get the world created.
'*Festina lente,* that's the thing, I won't be chicken-hearted,
'I've one outstanding candidate to get the party started.'

He scratched his wig, stuck out his neck,
And nominated David Peck.

Bazil carried his bat for 48 on the village green a year or two ago,
and kept goal at hockey. (It was only Lord Wolfenden who kept him
from a Blue, in 1973, aged sixty-seven.) A very remarkable man. It
was so sad when he went.

CHAPTER NINETEEN

Winged Words

Elizabeth loves entertaining, and in the summer, June Farm was full of friends from overseas. But it became painfully obvious that we couldn't keep on. Taylor gave notice as he could make more money clearing up in a factory than as a gardener, my original dailies had gone as soon as they got the old age pension, and Kent had a bad back. He didn't appear to hold with doctors, and thus there was no chance of improvement.

In 1969, only two years after we had spent all that money on improving the house, we decided that we must desert it. I was getting tired of commuting, and one wedding after another, each involving an immense amount of preparation and of hard work, left poor Elizabeth exhausted.

Elizabeth had a tiny house in Donne Place, Chelsea, but Papa would never be able to climb the stairs. It was very difficult. Only two years before, I had sworn that I would never throw the old boy out, and here was I thinking of telling him to find other headquarters. Both my sisters and my brother were prepared to have him, but he had his few belongings in my house, and he regarded it as his base, and the idea of leaving it was anathema. He went to live with John and my sister Lorna while we put the house up for sale. Then he had prostate trouble. At ninety-three. I know it is called the old man's disease but sixty is more commonly the time than ninety-three.

Our doctor said that in spite of his age he would be able to stand the operation. After a great deal of telephoning and so forth we got him into the Royal Masonic Hospital of which he was a patron. He was put in a ward with three other characters who were to have the same operation, and at first he did not seem dissatisfied. At last the specialist appeared and, according to Papa, it took him about thirty seconds to declare him inoperable. He was enraged, but, what was more important, we had to put him somewhere. Lorna was just going

163

to Guy's to be examined (they found that she had cancer of the lung, from which she died in the subsequent January), Sheila was in Jersey, and the old gentleman couldn't fly there, and Peter and Pam were abroad.

Elizabeth and I sat up all night trying to find a home for him, for he would need a night and day nurse and it was only a short time before we had to go on circuit. It was so pathetic; he had been the cynosure of all eyes at Philippa's wedding on 1st August and now, six weeks later, he had collapsed. He said that he couldn't see and couldn't hear, and I had had to take him all over the place to get the necessary appliances. He complained (and I don't blame him) about having to wear a catheter, a humiliating and revolting business.

It was Lorna who ultimately found a nursing home run by very kind people. He had his own room but declined to eat with the others saying that it was a geriatric ward. And so it was. It was miserable for him. At last we had to go to Leeds, promising him that he should spend Christmas with Lorna. He didn't know how ill she was, and John, Lorna's husband – who did know – nevertheless very sportingly said that he would have Papa, never mind how many nurses he had to have. And he prepared a wing of the house for him. But it was to no purpose. I was rung up at Leeds by the kind woman who was in charge of the nursing home. She was in tears. I was not. The poor old boy had died without pain having had a heart attack while talking to the doctor, and it was a good way to go. But I felt rather guilty that I was not in tears.

We found a little house in Walton Street, S.W.3 where we lived for six years. When we sold it we moved to Donne Place, where Jenny now resides as she has a general practice in Tooting. It is a very small house although marvellously situated. It really is ideal if you are away for most of the year as we were. When we were at home Elizabeth had what might almost be called a 'salon', but to be there all the year round would be unbearable.

Since Papa and Lorna died not a lot has happened to us. Sheila's daughter and Lorna's daughter have each produced two children. Elizabeth and I went to stay with Nigel in Teheran and visited Ispahan and Persepolis and, on our return journey, the dreaded Qum, where foreigners are unwelcome. Incredibly, I once won £250 from Ernie. Those were happy if humdrum years.

It was in 1971 that I got a letter from Quintin Hailsham asking me to be Chairman of a Committee to review the Law of Defamation.

I was rather flattered and accepted, and when he kindly allowed me some little say in the selection of the members I was more than pleased.

I had been out to grass for eight years and at last was to be allowed to come back to the subject I best understood. I was so excited that we immediately booked a return trip to the West Indies for the Long Vacation in a banana boat, with a sitting-room in which I could work.

And, by the time I returned, two enormous working-papers had been produced, and in my hubristic folly I imagined that this would be like old Chalmers doing the Sale of Gods Act and that I had nearly finished. The Committee when they met would agree with me, and there wouldn't be much point in hearing a lot of evidence.

I could not have been more wrong. It takes a very long time for important bodies to appoint a sub-committee to go into the matter carefully, and it is not easy to organise a meeting at a time convenient to a number of busy people. Some came to give evidence again and again. I think the Law Society came four times. One witness we certainly saw four times, and we had evidence, written or oral, from I don't know how many people. And, although I signed the report at Easter 1974, owing to strikes and one thing and another, it was not until March 1975 that it was published.

However, it was all tremendous fun. The committee were very keen and gave freely of their time and energy, some of them coming from great distances at much inconvenience. This particularly applied to Harry (Lord) Keith from Edinburgh and Bernard (Lord) Ballantrae from Ayrshire.

Betty Clarke, whom we have met before, came up from Benenden which must have been a toll upon a very busy headmistress who was also a JP, and Harman Grisewood, the father of the Third Programme, came up from Suffolk.

The Londoners were David Hirst, Peter Kimber, who is kindly publishing this book, Michael Rubinstein, who used to brief me a lot once upon a time, Bob Farmer of the Institute of Journalists, (whose battles in *The Times* newspaper with the National Union of Journalists are always a source of joy to me), one other, and myself.

'One other' was Harry Leon (Henry Cecil) who offered to look at this work for me. He was so busy with his broadcasting, novels and plays that I ought to have said, 'No, thank you'. But I thought that as a result it would emerge as clean as a whistle and more or less shorn of clichés (for I have retained some), and I said, 'Yes, please'.

They were a high-powered lot and I think that anyone who reads the report will think that I didn't do badly to achieve such agreement as was attained. My publisher in his defence of juries was Public Menace Number One, but in the nicest possible way, and we agreed to differ in the most urbane manner.

Bernard Ballantrae was Brigadier Sir Bernard Fergusson when I found that he was one of our number, and I read and was tremendously impressed by his autobiography *Trumpet in the Hall,* on my banana boat. I was honoured to have the great Chindit, who had been the king of the Palestine Police as well as Governor-General of New Zealand, on my committee. I knew that he was a literary man even if I knew little of any familiarity of his with the law of defamation.

Since he came on to my committee the most amazing things have happened to him. A life peerage, Chancellor of St Andrew's University, Chairman of the British Council, two stays as 'Your Grace' at Holyrood House and the Knighthood of the Thistle.

And Harry Keith started on the committee as The Hon H. S. Keith, QC and now as Lord Keith of Kinkel sits as a life peer in the supreme tribunal in the House of Lords, and should, by reason of his youth, one day preside over that august body.

Harry Leon is the only member to have died.

When, eventually, the report did appear we were lucky enough to escape criticism and even to obtain some modified applause for our exhausting efforts, with the inevitable comments that most of the reforms which we recommended were pretty obvious and long overdue, while the report was scarcely reformist in nature and had perhaps not gone far enough.

I am always amazed at the industry and intelligence of those who digest and comment authoritatively upon over three hundred printed pages on a complicated topic within twenty-four hours of publication. I imagine that the choice is either to read the report cursorily or not to read it at all, as it would no longer command any general interest by the time that it has been perused with care. Indeed, Lord Lloyd of Hampstead wrote a learned, interesting and complimentary article on the Report of the Committee on Defamation in a legal journal, of which he very kindly sent me a copy, but by the time that it arrived on my desk the Report seemed to be a thing of the past.

When Lord Goodman finished giving evidence to us, he said to me outside in the corridor after we had adjourned: 'Take my advice; you start it in the Lords.' I said, 'yes'.

From that I understood him to mean that our report would be

likely to be pigeon-holed unless we appended a draft statute to it, and that no Government would find the time to include it in its legislative programme, which nowadays often means undoing something that the enemy has done, or doing something which the enemy next time will undo. Of course, he may only have meant : 'Organise a debate upon your report in the Lords.' But how in the world do I do that as a mere puisne judge?

So, we decided to attach a draft statute and, finding that the Parliamentary draftsmen at Westminster were under tremendous pressure, engaged an expert in Edinburgh who served us excellently. But the matter never has been debated either in the House of Lords or in the House of Commons, and it is beginning to look as though it never will be. Mr Harold Wilson, as Prime Minister, once mentioned in an address to the Press at Liverpool that defamation was to be one of the subjects to be included in a Green Paper together with a number of other subjects concerning which no action has been taken, but nothing has happened.

Poor Harry Phillimore died before anything was done about his report on Contempt of Court. Governmental noises are at last being made about Section 2 of the Official Secrets Act on which Lord Franks and his committee reported in 1972, and happily Lord Franks is still with us. And I, too, would much like to think that those years of work were not wholly wasted. I was much cut down to size when recently I was dining at the High Table at my old college at Sidney Sussex, Cambridge, deep in conversation with the Master of Trinity Hall, the great legal college, and the very distinguished law Don of Sidney, who is an Honorary Bencher of my Inn, The Inner Temple, and the perennial subject of the dark complexities of the law of defamation became a matter of discussion. It was apparent, and indeed neither of these dignitaries made any bones about it, that they had never heard of my Committee, let alone its Report.

I was grumbling like this at the end of 1976 to my brother Tasker Watkins VC, and he said : 'But the Government will never do anything about that, Neville – defamation is a hot potato.' I don't know why it is a hot potato; I should have thought it absolutely non-political and possibly, even probably, not very important, except to lawyers and the Press. But if it is not very important, and the Government has other fish to fry, why appoint a Committee at all?

It used to be said that Committees and Royal Commissions were excellent devices, for the Government of the day, if harried on the topic, could blandly say that the matter was under review by the most eminent committee or commission, and that it would be very wrong to anticipate their findings. But who in the world is going to harry the government of the day as to whether, with television and broadcasting, the time has not come to abandon the anachronistic distinction between libel and slander altogether, and enact a single tort of defamation. The fact is that the law on this topic does need radical review as the Government realised in the 30's.

The Porter Committee, under Lord Porter, was appointed in March 1939, reported in October 1948, and the Defamation Act 1952, about which we were asked to report, only got on to the Statute Book at all because Mr Harold Lever, the present Chancellor of the Duchy of Lancaster, picked it up as a Private Members' Bill, which meant that it had to be rushed through on a Friday afternoon and that many valuable suggestions were lost by reason of lack of time.

Half-a-loaf is better than no bread, no doubt; but that is not what I would want.

I think that the House of Lords is a much more suitable body to deal with this recondite topic than the House of Commons and it should attract speeches from experienced and learned peers who know, or at least ought to know, what they are talking about. They all gave evidence before us, and one very eminent witness came down very heavily on one side of the fence on one topic, and then later clambered up and fell heavily off the fence on the other side, and asked me not to quote his earlier evidence in the report, which of course I did not.

So I was delighted when Viscount Hailsham, who incidentally had appointed the Committee, told me in 1975, that he would introduce the Bill in the Lords – 'Not this year, next year.' He is a man of absolute sincerity, and of course he meant it. And he has apologised to me since. I can understand what has happened. He has a job in the Shadow Cabinet, and this is not a political matter; he likes to think of himself as a lawyer as well as a politician and he sits often in the Privy Council, he really endures the heat and burden of the day in the Lords, particularly on matters of Nationalisation, and he has a nasty painful ankle. So all is forgiven.

But now we are in 1978. Who will help me? Any takers?

Gerald Gardiner, who continues to be a law reformer, but declines to sit, as a lawyer, on the Privy Council, tells me that his reforming body 'Justice' agrees with all our proposals except that of curtailing the use of juries. Of course, he is Chairman of the Open University, and 'Help the Aged', and all sorts of other things, and has not been made a Companion of Honour for nothing, and he is even older than I am. Perhaps he can find me a young and brilliant peer.

Possibly the Viscount Colville of Culross (whom I hasten to say that I have never met).

The Royal Commission on the Press has recently reported in July 1977. The late Mr Justice Morris Finer was Chairman until he died and would have done a wonderful piece of work on this difficult and fascinating topic which is indeed a political hot potato. And to many of us his selection didn't look good. A judge is of course expected to be impartial, independent and authoritative; then why select one who we all know will embody those three qualities, but who has in the past held strong and publicly expressed left-wing views and is still closely associated with the London School of Economics? But this Report to my mind is excellent, and I am so jealous of its panache.

The literary headings to each chapter I would have loved to have included in our Report. I did try, but when I read out an impassioned part of my chapter on juries referring to 'Chops and tomato sauce, members of the jury! Chops, gracious heavens, and tomato sauce!', there was a cry of 'What's all this about chops and tomato sauce?' and Charles Dickens, Mr Pickwick, Sergeant Buzfuz, Mrs Bardell, and Sir Neville Faulks were sunk without trace.

I managed to insert a quotation from Wordsworth's 'The Solitary Reaper' when no one was looking, and, I must confess, one of the newspaper critics picked it up, but I am afraid that our report although perhaps as interesting as that of Professor McGregor and his team was not as entertaining. He is so very right; unless a Blue Book is seen to be going to be entertaining reading, ninety-nine people out of a hundred turn to the Conclusions and Recommendations and then cannot find time to read the rest.

They seem to have had a few but not many jaunts abroad. We only had one, to Edinburgh, which I suppose was reasonable as we were considering the law of Scotland and it was only courteous to take the views of Scottish judges. I am sure that a number of my committee would much rather have been on the 'Think Tank', qualification for membership of which appears rather nebulous, except comparative youth, and have been able to go swanning all round the world, recommending the abolition of the British Council, and the trimming of the Diplomatic Service, rather than coming time after time to the Consultation Room in the Queen's Building in the Law

Courts and having to pay for a rather scratch lunch in the Crypt out of their own pockets.

One doesn't know what is going to happen to the recommendations of all these distinguished bodies, and whether their deliberations are to some extent a waste of time. The results of the Bullock commission were fairly predictable from the known view of the members. I don't myself think that anything will happen there, as their recommendations if implemented would only be overturned by the next Government.

At the moment my profession is the subject of a Royal Commission. We cannot tell what may be recommended. Maybe the fusion of the two professions which would in my view, and in that of all the judges, be disastrous – and that is the opinion of Chief Justice Warren Burger of the United States of America – where, as you know, the professions are already fused. Maybe they will recommend the abolition of the four Inns of Court, as to the history of two of which, the Inner and Middle Temples, I have already briefly animadverted. I do so hope not, although if these changes do come about they will be too late to affect me.

I have a slight suspicion that there is an atmosphere abroad to-day of reform for the sake of reform, and that a little more 'leave well alone' would not come amiss. I hope that that does not sound too political a remark; it is not meant to be so. But it is a fact of life that ancient mariners like myself are apt to resist radical change particularly if, as in my case, they have had a long and happy life getting happier with every year that passes.

It is equally a fact of life that there are some crusaders who however old they may be, like Gerald Gardiner, never lose their zest for reform. Infants are idealists and the old are realists. So that when Gerald Gardiner, as Lord Chancellor, appointed John Latey, a very dear man who has occupied the next room to me in the Law Courts for years and whom I would have bored with my company even more if his room did not smell like a smoking compartment in a commuter train, to inquire with other members of a committee into the Age of Majority he was, I am sure unwittingly, inquiring into the possibility of acquiring vast numbers of votes for Labour. Gerald has always held that if you are old enough to fight for your country you are old enough to have a vote. Personally I find that a gross over-simplification. Does this apply to pacifists like himself, and what fighting is a little girl at her desk at Benenden in the top form likely to be called upon to do? Predictably the majority gave the children the vote at 18 and the present Shadow Chancellor voted against it.

Reform for the sake of reform, say I, in an age of unprecedented teen-age hooliganism. But this reform was to the liking of the Government and there was to be no pigeon-holing this time. I have been thinking how it would have affected me all those years ago. I was eighteen on 27th January 1926 and had just been appointed a school praepostor and had an overblown sense of my own importance. But my creed was: 'Every child that is born alive must in fairness have the same opportunity in education', and I used to bore those few who were prepared to listen to me with these sentiments. General Election in January 1926? Faulks would unhesitatingly vote Socialist, his father Conservative, and his mother, because her father was a Liberal, Liberal. But a General Election some months later during the General Strike? And little Neville would unhesitatingly have cast his vote – simply out of sentiment – for Baldwin and Churchill. I don't think he ought to have had the vote at all.

But you can't put the clock back, as a distinguished Lord Justice once said to me when lamenting the final success of Gerald Gardiner and the late Sydney Silverman MP in their campaign for the abolition of Capital Punishment.

Lord Edmund-Davies, who is about eighteen months older than I am, stated in response to some valedictory observations on the occasion of his appointment as a Lord of Appeal in Ordinary, that, whereas crime was of course a grave and serious matter, he had sometimes enjoyed himself so much while exercising civil jurisdiction that he had found it almost indecent to accept his salary.

I think however that I should say that I am speaking on behalf of all the rest of my brethren when I say that I have found it entirely decent to accept my salary and only regret the effect of inflation thereon. The late Lord Parker once said to me, 'You know, my dear Neville, this question of judicial salaries is really most frightfully difficult. You see, there is George Brown saying, 'In the old days we used to pay them enormous sums to prevent them being corrupt. Now everybody knows that they aren't corrupt and that there's not the least chance of their being corrupt, so why on earth should we pay them any more money?' And some people, said the Lord Chief Justice, think that that is sense. I don't, but there it is.' And I wondered if Bridget's objections to my appointment had not been well-found after all.

During my illness I received a delightful 'get well' card signed by twenty-three High Court journalists. The message set out the understanding I have always had with the press: 'To Sir Neville Faulks. The under-signed High Court Scribes, missing your Lordship's eminently quotable judgments and your not-to-be-quoted asides, humbly petition your Lordship to *Get Well Soon* ! !'

Some time later I had a particularly squalid wife-swapping case which gave me an opportunity to repeat what I had earlier said about the meaning of Section 1(2)(a) of the Matrimonial Causes Act. No one had been in the least interested in my views, which was only to be expected, and on this occasion, not realising that the Press were in court, I told the parties that although I wasn't very enthusiastic about it, and would not have helped them under the old law when connivance and collusion were obstacles to divorce, I would give them their decrees because nowadays it appeared that all that they had to say was:— 'My wife has committed adultery, and – by the way – I find it intolerable to live with her because she wears pink knickers.' The word 'knickers' rather dated me, I thought, and I wished that I had been more modern in my vernacular. But the winged words had been uttered and they were all over the popular press. I didn't greatly object, for my friends wouldn't read about it, and I had found a platform for my views, strongly, even if wrongly, held.

But it didn't end there. I had temporarily and thank heaven, for the last time, – become 'news' again. Accordingly when, on the next day, I had a routine Jamaican defended cruelty before me, there was a reporter in court. Jamaicans appear to take the stigma of a divorce much more seriously than other ethnic groups and – however hopeless the case – will generally contest it. There was a lengthy opening address. It was a violence case and the petitioning wife was one of the many wonderful long-suffering Jamaican hospital nurses to whom we are accustomed in the Family Division.

I adjourned for luncheon, and had an idea. 'I am about to try a stupendously boring defended cruelty where the husband is a Chelsea dustman,' I said to my neighbour. 'Do you think that if I looked very serious, and enquired whether, as we had had a lot of trouble in Chelsea with the dustmen lately, perhaps the husband would rather be tried by another judge who was not a resident in the Royal Borough, I should have any luck?' 'Well, you never know,' he replied. 'You might.'

He was wrong. I made my enquiry solemnly, as if at a funeral. And the husband slapped his thighs and laughed and laughed. He ignored his counsel, and stood up and shouted: 'No objection.' So on we went with the case. I found against him solemnly and without a smile; he appeared neither surprised or displeased. We finished the case by the end of the day by dint of my having kept entirely silent.

And next day the readers of a national newspaper read: 'Pink knickers Judge slams dustmen.' This led some gentleman in a Sunday popular newspaper, perhaps short of material, to enquire: 'Why doesn't Mr Justice Faulks shut up?' I was amused but Elizabeth was not. I told her that these things were a nine-day wonder. But she was right, for I picked up my *Times* newspaper and started to read it in bed in the following November, and page 2 recorded the annual meeting of some body connected with the solicitors' profession. (Not the Law Society.)

It seemed that someone from the Midlands had called for a petition to the Lord Chancellor for my removal on the grounds that I had used the words 'pink knickers' and also because I was an unkind judge having called someone a villain. I was a little bit upset about that as I am not unkind and do not make a habit of calling people 'villains'. He lost, I am happy to say. But that did make me realise that a good judge must be both incognito and incommunicado. Since then all my work has been carried out in chambers, the male equivalent of purdah, and, if I have ever said anything witty, which is not admitted, no one has been allowed to report it.

Gentle reader, if you have ploughed through these two volumes – and I congratulate you if such be the case – you will have observed that my life has been one of ups and downs. A hopeful start, an undistinguished war, ten years on the treadmill, three years when, as dear Mr Justice (Alan) Mocatta once said, 'You were a household word' and, thereafter, fifteen years of obscurity.

Those years were uneventful and, you may think, unsuccessful. For I never soared to the Court of Appeal or to the Lords. But how could it be otherwise? In the Family Division all the matters which we have to decide, are matters of fact, not of law. I have never been tempted to say that where little Tommy should spend his summer holidays involved a point of law so that I should adjourn the matter for my judgment into open court. I take the view that the customers want to know the form; they want to know it quickly; and they want to know it cheaply.

I have, in the fifteen years, before I retired, delivered three (3) – in case the number may be misunderstood – reserved judgments. A reserved judgment is a bore to oneself because it is unnecessary labour and unless it is very complicated, surely, one, as a High Court Judge, ought to be able to do it off the cuff – and it is a bore to the poor customers, who want to know the school solution. Who's won? is the cry – not whether the judge has expressed himself with remarkable lucidity.

One of the three reserved judgments was Novotnik, (which I mentioned on page 156). The second was on the same theme where I dissented from Jack Simon and Roger Ormrod, and I thought, of course, that I was right. And the third was a matter of such moment that I cannot recollect it at all. It's an entirely different cup of tea in the Court of Appeal, to which, thank Heaven, I was never bidden. There the work never ends, and reserved judgments are lying at home to be threshed into good English prose after your spouse has gone to bed. And at the same time you are hearing something fantastically obscure with two or three other matters on your mind. This is not sour grapes. I agree that for the last fifteen years I have not had much opportunity to use my 'tiny mind', as Mr Healey would say, but my physical disabilities would have made it impossible to sit with two others in the Court of Appeal had I ever been invited. Indeed, the Clerk of the Rules in the Family Division has known that I cannot bear the Divisional Court (two old gentlemen in wigs, etc.) unless it cannot be avoided.

I have an opinion with which many of my brethren may not be in accord. It is quite simple. It is this. At the moment the law is that a High Court Judge does not have to retire until he is seventy-five years of age. He cannot retire on full pension until (a) he has served for fifteen years, or (b) has attained the age of seventy, in which he can only get the proportion of his pension attributable to the number of completed years he has served, or (c) he has a medical certificate to say that it would be injurious to his health to soldier on, in which case the proportionate allotment applies. Circuit judges are subject to similar rules except that they have to go at seventy-two instead of seventy-five, although there is a discreet – and proper – little proviso that the Lord Chancellor may let them go on until they are seventy-four. Why a Circuit Judge should be expected to become gaga before a High Court Judge is an interesting question. Indeed, Lords Evershed and Jenkins got into difficulties late in their careers, while those of humbler standing appear to have been unaffected.

I think that all puisne judges should be compelled to go at seventy. If they have been bright enough to get to the Court of Appeal before then, by all means let them go on to seventy-five. Of course, a gate at seventy might shut out someone brilliant and in the plenitude of his powers, but then the Master of the Rolls could still invite this hypothetical person to sit in the Court of Appeal as he has done in the cases of Sir John Pennycuick, lately Vice-Chancellor, and of Sir David Cairns.

I went before I was seventy. Surely there must have been someone of fifty-five who could do the job more efficiently. There are exceptions, but it is better to make a rule than to keep judges on who know that they will be so bored that they will die if and when they retire. That is not the way to obtain the very high standard of justice of which in Britain we are so proud.

I do not expect to be remembered. Perhaps a few may have read these not very literary effusions. Perhaps someone may recollect *Rookes* v *Barnard*. But there is a good deal more of me in the Law Reports as an advocate than as a judge.

But there is a lot of donkey-work to be done, by a judge and that doesn't find it's way into print. When I was at the Bar there was a dear old bachelor judge known as 'Foul-mouthed Finnemore', because he was the President of the Boys' Brigade, and never used a rude word in his life. He was known to be quick, polite, and fair, and he never advanced to the Court of Appeal. I have tried to emulate him and have not set my sights higher than that. If I have managed that I am content.

I thought that I had finished what poor Harry Leon would have called 'the second draft', and I went out on to the landing and met Elizabeth who was emerging from the bathroom with, somewhat unexpectedly, a shopping basket in her hand.

'Darling, the great work is done.'

'Oh good. I'm just going to get the tea cups for Annie.'

For there is a christening tomorrow, and that new life is a great deal more important than this old one.

Postscript

Readers of *No Mitigating Circumstances* may be interested to know that Uncle Sydney failed to complete playing the Grieg Piano Concerto on his ninety-eighth birthday. His son Barry thought that rather disappointing. I thought he did rather well to get as far as he did before tiring.

SOME PRESS NOTICES OF
NO MITIGATING CIRCUMSTANCES

'A treasure chest of brilliant story telling and legal gems.'
JEAN ROOK in the *Daily Express*

'Hilariously entertaining autobiography.'
GRAHAM LORD in the *Sunday Express*

'Elevation to the bench sometimes has a dehumanizing effect:
not so in the case of Sir Neville Faulks. His autobiography *No
Mitigating Circumstances* is consistently genial: it generates a
strong current of euphoria. The style is positively jaunty especially
when describing his relations:

> My paternal grandfather was apparently a rather success-
> ful milkman. . . My cousin Philip looked much more like
> Billy Bunter than an embryo criminal. . . He decided that
> the life for him was a life of crime. He chose burglary.

'Sir Neville was engaged in several libel cases. . . He also appeared
in two famous literary cases of the period. One was *Honor Tracy*
v *The Sunday Times*. The other was *Evelyn Waugh* v *Nancy
Spain and the Daily Express*. . . Another breakfast-table-enlighten-
ing case was the *Marchioness of Winchester* v *Mrs Fleming*
(mother of Ian and Peter). We leave him on the verge of taking
silk, an agreeable-sounding person, modest about his own abilities,
and free from any trace of legal pomposity.'
MAURICE RICHARDSON in *The Times Literary Supplement*

Illustrated £5.50 net

Index

Ackner, Mr Justice, 86, 87
Adams, Dr Bodkin, 38
Aldous, Guy, 79
Alexander, Field Marshal Earl, 65
Algarve, 191
Algeciras, 122
Allenby, Lord, 140
An Army in Exile, 60
An Inspector Calls, 23
Anders, General Wladyslaw, 59-67, 68, 69, 90
Andrade, Professor Edward, 71, 72
Anne, HRH The Princess, 142
Appleton, Sir Edward, 71
Armstrong-Jones, Ronald, 56
Arnold, Mr Justice, 73
Ashworth, Mr Justice, 66
Atlanta, 47, 52
Attlee, Clement, 77
Auschwitz, 61
Australia, 94

Bagnall, Mr Justice, 79
Baker, Sir George, 158
Baldwin, Stanley, 171
Balfour, Jabez, 18
Ballantrae, Lord, 164, 166
Bank Rate Tribunal, 105
Barnard, Mr, 95
Baron, Herbert, 24
Barr, Joanne Rio, 31
Barr, Mr Justice, 70
Barrington, 52
Barry, Mr Justice, 33, 71, 118

Bassey, Shirley, 55
Beaverbrook, Lord, 98
Beaverbrook Newspapers, 90, 98
Beeching, Lord, 162
Beirut, 54
Benenden School, 135, 142, 144, 146, 170
Beney, Fred, 122
Berkeley, Humphrey, 90
Berlin, 18
Betchworth, 61
Beyfus, Gilbert, 26, 27, 28, 29, 113
Birkenhead, Lord, 162
Birkett, Lord, 38, 140, 143
Birley, Colonel, 141
Birmingham, 91, 93, 132, 133
Blackpool, 55
Blackstone, Sir William, 68, 69, 70
Bligh, Tim, 128
Blum, R. C. de M., 72
BOAC, 94, 95, 96, 102
Bogusz-Szysko, General, 64
Boulton, Sir William, 49, 77
Bourne, Dr Aleck, 41, 42
Bowring, C. T. & Co. Ltd., 124
Brabin, Mr Justice, 12, 112, 113
Bradford, Lord, 144
Bridge, Lord Justice, 160
Brighton, 75
Bristow, Mr Justice, 59, 90
Brothers in Law, 9
Buchanan, Jack, 53
Buckmaster, Lord, 77
Burger, Chief Justice Warren, 170

Bush, Major Anthony, 153
Bush, Philippa, 153, 154, 164

Cairns, Lady, 131
Cairns, Lord Justice, 71, 120, 131, 175
Caldecote, Lord, 97
Cambridge, 14, 50, 70, 102, 122, 167
Campobasso, 60
Canada, 50, 56, 57
Cannon, Mr, 98
Carr, Isobel, 153
Carr, Richard, 135, 152, 153, 154
Carson, Sir Edward, 162
Carter, Barry, 130
Casement, Sir Roger, 12
Castro, Dr, 88, 89
Cassandra, *see* Connor, Bill
Cassels, Mr Justice, 34, 150
Chaplain, Charlie, 26
Chapple, Mr, 98
Charles, Mr Justice, 99
Cecil, Henry *see* Leon, His Honour H. C.
Cheltenham, 131
Chicago, 47
Churchill, Randolph, 46, 47
Churchill, Sir Winston, 26, 62, 63, 64, 81, 106, 171
Clark, Sir Andrew, QC, 101
Clarke, Annie, 153, 175
Clarke, Miss Betty, MA, JP, 144, 165
Clarke, Lt Cdr John, 153
Clements, His Honour Judge, 155
Cohen, Lady, 114
Cohen, Lord, 114
Collingwood, Mr Justice, 126, 127, 132
Collins, Canon L. G., 136
Colville of Culross, Lord QC, 169
Conduct and Etiquette at the Bar, 77
Connor, Sir William (Cassandra)

26-31
Co-operative News, 78
Coldstream, Sir George, 116
Corbishley, S. J., Father, 14
Cotes-Preedy, Pat, 52
Coulson, Stuart, 68
Courtneidge, Dame Cicely, 29, 53
Cow, Noel, 23
Crawley, Cosmo, 125
Crossman, Richard, 129
Cuba, 88, 89
Cudlipp, Lord (Hugh), 28, 29, 30
Cumming-Bruce, Lord Justice, 70
Cuneo, Terence, 140
Cunningham, George, MP, 97, 98
Cunningham, Sir Knox, QC, MP, 15
Curtis-Bennett, Derek, 15
Curtis-Bennett, Sir Henry, 15, 16
Cyprus, 81
Czechoslovakia, 136

Daily Express, 43, 70
Daily Mail, 91, 92, 100, 106, 107, 108, 109, 128, 135
Daily Mirror, 26, 27, 29
Daily Sketch, 93
Daily Telegraph, 104, 106, 107, 108, 109, 110, 126, 127
Daily Worker, 88
Dale, Sir Henry, 71
Daniels, David, 35, 37, 124
Daniels, Zena, 32, 34, 35, 36, 37
Darling, Lord, 12, 74
Dartmouth, 148
Davidson, Hugh, 105, 110
Davies, Lord Justice Arthian, 84, 85
Dawson & Co., 146
Defamation, Committee on, 9, 66, 108, 164-169
Denning, Lord, 45, 86, 131, 156, 160
Devlin, Lord, 38, 74, 87, 103
Dickens, Charles, 15

Dickens, Sir Henry, 15
Dickinson, James, QC, 56
Dilhorne, Lady, 144
Dilhorne, Lord, 120, 125, 126, 127,
    130, 137, 142
Diplock, Lord, 33, 78, 137
Dodson, Gerald, 16
Donaldson, Mr Justice, 79, 131
Donovan, Lady, 103
Donovan, Lord, 80, 84, 103
Doughty, Charles, QC, MP, 121
Dunboyne, Lord, 129, 130
Duncan, Colin, QC, 33, 46, 55,
    101, 103, 105, 122
Dundee, Lord, 148
Dunlop Rubber Co. Ltd., 92, 93
Dunn, Mr Justice, 93
Du Parcq, Lord, 52

Edinburgh, 91, 165, 169
Edmund-Davies, Lord, 171
Eisenhower, President, 38
Electrical Trades Union, 98
Elizabeth II, HM The Queen,
    117, 128, 129, 140
Elizabeth, HRH The Queen
    Mother, 140
Ely Brewery Co. Ltd., 18
Engineering and Shipbuilding
    Draughtsmen, Association of,
    94, 95, 96, 100, 101
English Electric, 96
Eveleigh, Mr Justice, 56
Evershed, Lord, 87, 174
Exeter, 118

Falmouth, Lord, 71
Falmouth, 135
Farmer, Bob, 165
Farden, Colonel Cyril, 140
Faulks, Barry, 177
Faulks, Lady (Bridget), 28, 33, 47,
    48, 49, 50, 51, 82, 102, 112, 113,
    115, 117, 118, 120, 121, 122,
    123, 126, 127, 128, 130, 131,
    132, 133, 134-5, 139, 147, 171

Faulks, Caroline, 153
Faulks, Edward, 157
Faulks, Lady (Elizabeth), 9, 10, 30,
    122, 136, 140, 144-155, 156, 163,
    164, 173, 175
Faulks, Esmond, 122, 127, 135,
    154
Faulks, Judith, 120, 122, 127, 130,
    132, 135, 142, 143, 144, 145, 154
Faulks, Lorna, *see*
    Radington-Meech
Faulks, Major James (Papa) 73,
    112, 120, 121, 123, 127, 132,
    135, 140, 149, 151, 152, 163
Faulks, Nigel, 122, 127, 135, 152,
    164
Faulks, Peter and Pamela, 141,
    143, 157, 164
Faulks, Sheila, *see* Lee
Faulks, Sydney (Uncle) 73, 152,
    177
Fearnley-Whittingstall, Bill, QC,
    46
Financial Times, The, 36
Finchfort Publishers Ltd, 35, 36,
    37
Finer, Mr Justice Morris, 23, 169
Finkelbaum, Joseph P., 47, 49, 50,
    51, 68, 77, 102, 112
Finnemore, Mr Justice, 175
Fisher, Mr Justice, 117
Fistal, Mr, 95, 96
Fleming, Mrs, 51
Fleming, Sergeant, 75, 76, 77, 78
Fletcher, Mr, 152
Forsyth, Bruce, 53, 55, 68
Fort William, 92
Foster, Mary, 131
Foulkes, Mr, 98
Franks, Lord, 167
Fraser on Libel, 82

Gaitskell, Hugh, 19, 78
Gardiner, Lord CH, 28, 29, 30,
    32, 33, 35, 38, 46, 58, 59, 82, 88,

89, 90, 98, 101, 102, 103, 113, 123, 124, 168, 170, 171
Gas, Adam, 60, 61
George VI, HM King, 59
George-Brown, Lord, 171
Georgetown, 50
Germany, 18
Gibraltar, 63, 122
Gloucester, 118, 132
Glyndebourne, 39
Goddard, Lord, 118
Goldsworthy, Mr, 108
Gollancz, Victor, 20
Gombos, Laszlo, 51
Goodhart, Professor, 148
Goodman, Lord, 166
Gordon Dadds & Co, 41
Gordon Hotels, 32-37, 96
Gorman, Mr Justice, 118
Graz, 60
Green, Mr and Mrs, 149
Greene, Lady, 114
Greene, Lord, 114
Gregory, Sir Holman, 15
Griffiths, Mr Justice, 56
Grisewood, Harman, 165
Grundig (Great Britain) Ltd, 71-75
Grunwald, Mr, 17, 18, 19, 21, 22, 23
Guest, Anne, 136
Guest, Ronald, 136
Gulbenkian, Nubar, 45

Haakon, HM King, 135
Hailsham, Lord, 12, 34, 164, 168
Haldane, Lord, 24
Halsbury, Lord, 71
Hamilton, Mrs, 120, 135
Hamilton, William, MP, 28
Hamson, Professor, QC, 50, 102
Hanbury, Professor, 48
Harman, Lord Justice, 72, 73, 84, 85, 101
Harris, Sir Ronald, 144

Hastings, Sir Patrick, 38, 143
Havers, Mr Justice, 116, 121, 122, 131
Havers, Sir Michael, 121, 122
Harvey, Cyril, QC, 119
Hatry, Clarence, 17
Havana, 89
Haw-Haw, Lord, 86
Hawke, Sir Anthony, 15
Hawkins, Lionel, 45, 56
Hazell, Mr, 98
Heald, Sir Lionel, QC, 45, 56, 114
Healey, Rt Hon Denis, 173
Heathrow Airport, 94, 95, 99
Herbert Oppenheimer, Nathan & Vandyk, 56, 57
Heseltine, E. G., 59, 65
Heuston, Professor, 69
Hexham, 122
Hewart, Lord, 44
Hewson, Mr Justice, 130, 132
High Wycombe, 68
Hilbery, Sir Malcolm, 139
Hill v *Hill*, 102
Hip Foong Hong v *H. Neotia & Co*, 77
Hirst, David, QC, 22, 43, 55, 56, 69, 73, 107, 110, 165
Hitler, Adolf, 58, 60, 62, 63, 65, 139, 140
Hobson, John, QC, 112, 113
Hochhuth, Rolf, 62, 63
Hodgson, Mr Justice, 43
Hodson, Lord, 87
Hogg, Sir Douglas, (Viscount Hailsham) 12
Holland, Sir Milner, QC, 32, 101, 113
Hopkinson, Mr, 142
Howard, Mr Justice, 123
Hughes, Richard, 122
Hulbert, Jack, 29, 53
Hume-Williams, Sir Ellis, 122
Humphreys, Mr Justice, 14
Huntley v *Thornton* 1957, 101

Hyams v *Stuart King,* 102
Hylton Foster, Sir Harry, QC, 81, 114

India, 91
Indianapolis, 143
Inglesia, Mr, 88
Ispahan, 164
Israel, 17, 19
It's in the Bag, 70

Jackson, Leonard Percival, 32, 34, 35, 96, 101
Jacobs, David, 54, 55
Jasper, Harry Oscar, 18, 19, 21, 22, 23, 24, 32, 68, 71
Jenkins, Lord, 17
Jewish Chronicle, 90
John o'Groats, 92
Joseph, Maxwell, 20
Jowitt, Earl, 126
June Farm, 60, 70, 83, 116, 120, 140, 149, 151, 163

Karminski, Mr Justice, 130
Keith, Lord, 165, 166
Kennedy, President John, 49
Kent, Mr and Mrs, 151, 153
Kerr, Mr Justice, 55
Keyes, Lord, 32-37, 44, 66, 82, 112, 113
Kilmuir, Lord, 14, 15, 120
Kimber, William, (Peter) 11, 12, 165, 166
King, Cecil, 129
King Lear, 151
Kirkwood, Andrew, 142, 143, 144, 145, 153
Kirkwood, Jenny, 52, 154
Kirkwood, Tristram, 145, 146, 147, 154
Klimkowski, Captain, 63
Kot, Professor Stanislaw, 62, 64
Kwiatowski, Mr, 60, 61

Lady Chatterley's Lover, 47
Land's End, 92, 93
Langton, Mr Justice, 155
The Last Serjeant, 12
Latey, Mr Justice, 170
Law, Harry, 52
Law Quarterly Review, 74
Lawrence, Mr Justice, 38-52, 70, 113
Lawson, Mr Justice, 84, 85, 86, 103, 112, 113
Lauder, Sir Henry, 53
Lawton, Lord Justice, 32, 33, 160
Lee, Sheila, 164
Leeds, 9, 35, 164
Leigh, 60
Leigh, Vivien, 61
Leno, Dan, 53
Leon, His Honour H. C., 10, 11, 165, 175
Lens, 61
Lever, Harold, MP, 167
Lewes, 38
Lewis, John, 67, 104-105, 106, 107, 108, 110, 111
Lewis & Lewis, 59, 60
Lewis v *Associated Newspapers,* 90, 107-111
Lewis v *Daily Telegraph,* 90, 104-107
Lewis Silkin & Partners, 98, 100
Liberace, 26-31, 46, 54
Liberace, Salvatore, 27
Lincoln, 149, 150
Lincoln, Ashe, 34, 35, 37, 124
Liverpool, 9, 92
Lloyd, Lord, 166
Lloyd-Jones, Mr Justice, 157, 158
Liversidge v *Anderson,* 86
Lives of the Lord Chancellors, 69
Lochhead, R. K., 24
Los Angeles, 31
Lynskey Tribunal, 88

Maclaren, Leon, 72

McCrindle, R. A., QC, 55
McGregor, Lord, 169
MacKenna, Mr Justice, 116, 131
Macmillan, Harold, OM, 18, 19,
　120, 128
McNair, Sir William, 55, 93
Macnaughten, Mr Justice, 41
MacPherson, Aimee Semple, 27
Malone, Herbert, QC, 112, 113
Mann, Mr, 88, 89
Manningham-Buller, Sir Reginald,
　(*see* Dilhorne, Lord,) 115, 120
Marshall, Mr Justice, 116
Marshall-Hall, Sir Edward, QC,
　15
Mars-Jones, Mr Justice, 48
Mars-Jones, Lady (Sheila) 48
Meek, Mr, 75, 76, 78, 107
Meek v *Fleming,* 75-8, 80
Megarry, (Vice-Chancellor) 12
Megaw, Lord Justice, 55, 124
Melford Stevenson, Mr Justice, 38,
　55, 131
Melton Mowbray, 37
Merton, Sir Thomas, 71
Mihailovich, General, 60
Mikolajczck, Mr, 61, 63
Milburn, The Very Rev R. L. P.,
　153
Milmo, Mr Justice, 26, 32, 53, 59,
　70, 93, 105, 106, 107, 108, 137
Mocatta, Lady, 133
Mocatta, Mr Justice, 73, 133, 173
Monkhouse, Bob, 29
Monte Carlo, 114, 56
Monte Cassino, 59, 65
Montreal, 47, 48, 56
Moore, Dr Barbara, 91-3
Morris of Borth-y-Gest, Lord, 87,
　109, 110
Morrison, Herbert, MP, 59
Morton of Henryton, Lord, 114
Moscow, 61, 62, 64
Mosley, Sir Oswald, 98, 99
Mould, Mrs, 120

Muggeridge, Malcolm, 28
Murray, Mr, 17, 18, 21, 22, 23, 24

Nabarro, Sir Gerald, 46
Napley, Sir David, 23
Newcastle, 9, 154
New York, 48, 56, 57
Nidditch, Lazarus, 18
Nixon, ex-President Richard, 49
Norwich, 122, 127
Nottingham, 29
Notting Hill Riots, 30
Novotnik, Mr and Mrs, 156, 173
Nutt, Mr, 34, 35, 36, 37

Observer, The, 47, 113, 114
O'Connor, Mr Justice, 56
Odgers, Charlotte, 135
Odgers, Miriam, 135, 143
Oppenheimer, Nathan & Vandyk,
　Messrs, 56, 57
Ormerod, Lord Justice, 73, 74
Ormrod, Lord Justice, 56, 73, 173
Oxford, 56, 68, 69, 70, 145, 148,
　149, 154

Parham, The Right Rev Arthur,
　Bishop of Reading, 146, 147,
　148, 150
Paris, 47
Parker, Commander Michael, 89
Parker of Waddington, Lord, 117,
　118, 171
Patino, Mr, 66
Paull, Mr Justice, 24, 56, 114
Pazos, Senor, 89
Pearce, Lord, 76, 84, 85, 109, 140,
　155
Pearson, Lord, 43, 74, 126
Peck, His Honour Judge, 160, 162
Peculiarities of the Temple, The,
　140
Pennycuick, Sir John, 175
Persepolis, 164
Persia, 59, 62

Philip, HRH The Prince, 128, 140
Phillimore, Lord Justice, 14, 70,
    142, 143, 145, 155, 167
Pilot Insurance Co, 24
Pilsudski, Marshal, 59
Platts-Mills, John, QC, 56
Poole, 153
Popill, Mr, 63
Poland, 62, 64
Porter, Lord, 168
Presenzano, 65
Prior, Oliver, 122
Pritt, Denis, QC, 97
Proops, Miss Marjorie, 30
Purley, 33

Queen Mary, HMS, 23, 48

Radington-Meech, John, 135, 164
Radington-Meech, Lorna, 19, 135,
    163, 164
Rank, Lord, 23, 64
Rawalpindi, 122
Rawlinson, Sir Peter, 15, 24, 58-67,
    121
Rawson, Sir Stanley, 89, 90
Rayden on Divorce, 126
Reading, 154
Reading, Bishop of, *see* Parham
Reading, Marquess of, 24
Redman, General Sir Harold, 144
Rees, Mr Justice, 83, 112, 113, 127
Reid, Lord, 80, 86, 87, 96, 103,
    110
Reigate, 22, 120, 135
Rex v *Joyce*, 86
Reynolds, Quentin, 20
Rhodesia, 85
Richards, Sir Norman, QC, 143
Riches, Right Rev Kenneth, 149,
    153
Riches, Katherine, 149
Richmond, Virginia, 47, 52
Ridge, Chief Constable, 80, 83, 84,
    85, 86, 96

Ridge v *Baldwin*, 80
Roberts-Wray, Sir Kenneth, QC,
    14
Robinson, Eric, 72
Roche, Hon T. G., QC, 112
Romer, Count Adam, 63
Rookes, Douglas, 94, 95, 96, 97,
    98, 99, 100, 101, 103
Rookes v *Barnard*, 73, 90, 94-103,
    105, 124, 174
Roskill, Lord Justice, 55, 74, 137
Roskill, Sir Ashton, 138
Rothermere, Lord, 120, 127
Rowing William, 134
Rubber Improvements Ltd, 104,
    105, 106, 107
Rubinstein, Michael, 165
Rubinstein Nash and Co, 47
Russell, Harold, 52
Russell, Lady, 48
Russell of Killowen, Lord, 24
Russia, 59, 61, 62, 63, 91
Russell, Bertrand, 143

Sachs, Lord Justice, 99, 102
Sachs, Solly, 90
Saint Valery en Caux, 68
Salmon, Lady, 30
Salmon, Lord, 30, 37, 107
Salmond on Torts, 69
San Severo, 81
Scarman, Lord, 73, 131
Schonfeld, Rabbi, 17
Scrutton, Lord Justice, 13
Scrutton on Charter-parties, 25
Sebag Shaw, Lord Justice, 75, 76,
    77
Sellers, Lord Justice, 44, 103
Semprini, 28
Shannon, 48
Shawcross, Lord, 101
Sheldon, Dr, 135
Shell Petroleum, 88, 89
Sherek, Henry, 70

Sikorski, General, 60, 61, 62, 64, 65, 66
Sikorski, Madam, 63
Silkin, Rt Hon John, 97, 98
Silkin, Lewis and Partners, 98
Silkin, Lord, 97
Silkin, Rt Hon Sam, 97, 103
Silsoe, Lord, 140, 144
Silverman, Sydney, MP, 171
Silverthorne, Mr, 95
Simon, Lord of Glaisdale, 72, 74, 130, 174
Skelhorn, Sir Norman, QC, 23
Slade, Gerald, (Mr Justice) 22, 32, 82
Slater, Jim, 18
Slaughter and May, 90
Slesser, Lord Justice, 73
Soldiers, The, 62
Soskice, Frank, *see* Stow Hill, Lord
Speed, Sir Robert, QC, 19, 22
Stalin, 62
Stable, Lady Wintringham, 132, 133
Stable, Mr Justice Wintringham, 84, 85, 132, 133, 142, 143, 146, 150
Stamp, Lord Justice, 160
Stanley, Mr, 88
State Building Society, 18, 23
Steele, Mrs, 53, 54
Steele, Tommy, 53, 54, 55, 68, 72
Stoke D'Abernon, 144
Stoke Fleming, 149
Stow Hill, Lord, 33, 56. 78
Streatfeild, Mr Justice, 57, 83
Sullivan, Mr, 55
Sullivan, Serjeant, 12, 13, 97
Sunday Dispatch, 19, 55
Sunday Express, 90
Sunday Pictorial, 29
Sunday Times, 29
Sutton, Air Marshal Sir Bertine, 148
Sutton-Scott-Tucker, Juliet and

Michael, 148, 149
Swift, Mr Justice Rigby, 12
Switzerland, 91

Tasker Watkins, Mr Justice, VC, 167
Taylor, Dr, 130
Taylor, Mr, 120, 135, 163
Teheran, 152, 164
Terrell, Stephen, QC, 59
Thalben-Ball, Dr George, CBE, 119
Theodore Goddard & Co, 51
Thompson, Mr Justice, 99, 124
Times, The, 23, 24, 33, 36, 45, 54, 64, 79, 80, 86, 103, 126, 127, 129, 135, 145, 146, 160, 165, 173
Tracy, Miss Honor, 24, 29, 66
Trade, Board of, 22, 23, 32, 75
Trieste, 60
Trumpet in the Hall, 166
Twelfth Night, 140

Uppingham School, 125, 130, 135, 156

Vandervell, Mr,
Vassall Tribunal, 126
Virginia, 47, 52

Wade, Professor, 14
Walsh, Dennis, 44
Warsaw, 60, 61, 63, 65
Washington, 47, 48, 49, 51, 52
Waugh, Evelyn, 66
Waugh v *Spain,* 98
Wedderburn, Lord, 102, 103
West Indies, 165
Whitehouse, Mrs, 155
Whitmore, Francis, 105
Widgery, Lord Chief Justice, 90
Wild, Sir Ernest, 15
Williams, Kenneth, 128
Williams, Harold and Dottie, 52
Willink, Rt Hon Sir Henry, 56

Wilson, Sir Harold, KG, 167
Winchester, 116, 118, 119, 120,
 121, 122, 139
Winchester, Lady, 51, 75
Wingate-Saul, His Honour Judge,
 12, 145, 160, 162
Winn, Lord Justice, 98

Wisconsin, 27
Wittenham House, 149, 152
Wolfit, Sir Donald, 121
Woodcock, George, 100
Worcester, 118

York, 81